FINGS AIN
THEY USED T'BE

A play by
FRANK NORMAN

Lyrics by
LIONEL BART

SAMUEL FRENCH

LONDON

NEW YORK   TORONTO   SYDNEY   HOLLYWOOD

ISBN 0 573 08045 3

Enquiries regarding the music should be made to Samuel French Ltd

FINGS AIN'T WOT THEY USED T'BE

First performed by Theatre Workshop under the direction of Joan Littlewood at the Theatre Royal, Stratford, E.15, on February 17th, 1959.

The first West End production was at the Garrick Theatre on Thursday, February 11th, 1960, with the following cast:

Frederick Cochran	Glynn Edwards
Lily Smith	Miriam Karlin
Paddy	Paddy Joyce
Sergeant Collins	Tom Chatto
Policewoman	Yootha Joyce
Police Constable	George Sewell
Betty	Toni Palmer
Rosey	Barbara Windsor
Tosher	James Booth
Redhot	Edward Caddick
The Brass Upstairs	Yootha Joyce
Horace Seaton	Wallace Eaton
Gamblers and **Builders**	George Sewell
	Michael O'Brien
	Rick Morgan
	Louis Adams
	Neville Munroe
Percy Fortesque	Wallas Eaton
Myrtle	Yootha Joyce
Busker	George Sewell
Teddy Girls and **Boys**	Margaret Russell
	Mary Sheen
	Barbara Cording
	Norman Gunn
	James Dark
	Tamba Allen
	Ian Laing
A "Mystery"	Mary Sheen
A Priest	Wallas Eaton

MUSICAL NUMBERS

Prologue
G' Night Dearie   Collins, Police Constables
                                     Betty and Rosey

ACT I
Fings Ain't Wot They Used T'Be   Lil, Fred
Layin' Abaht   Tosher, Rosey, Lil, Fred,
                                 Redhot and Company
Where It's Hot   Redhot
The Ceiling's Comin' Dahn   Lil, Paddy, Company
Contempery   Horace, Mystery, Tosher,
                                 George and Company

ACT II
Cochran Will Return   Fred and Company
Polka Dots   Lil, Horace, Tosher, Paddy and
                                 Company
Where Do Little Birds Go?   Rosey
Big Time   Norman
Things Aren't What They Used
    To Be (reprise)   Percy, Myrtle
Carve Up   Norman and the Teds
Cop A Bit of Pride   Collins, Betty and Company
The Student Ponce   Tosher, Norman, Teds
Fings Ain't Wot They Used T'Be (reprise)   Company

INTRODUCTION

by Joan Littlewood

In the theatre of those dear departed days when every actress had roses round her vowels, and a butler's suit was an essential part of an actor's equipment, the voice of the Cockney was one long whine of blissful servitude. No play was complete without its moronic maid or faithful batman—rich with that true cockney speech and humour learned in the drama schools.

This refined and treasured theatre could not attract nor touch the vulgar populace, our theatres were kept pure and innocent, with the charm of an aged Peter Pan.

Frank Norman had never seen such plays, nor even been in a theatre, when he wrote *Fings Ain't Wot They Used T'Be*. If he had he would probably have run for his life. His first venture into any theatre was at Stratford, with the first draft of his own play.

With a true instinct for theatre he worked as a playwright must, in collaboration with the actors, and with Lionel Bart the composer. New ideas, arising out of rehearsal were drafted into the text, until an entertainment was produced which packed our theatre night after night with cockney people, most of whom, like Frank Norman, had never been in a theatre in their lives.

AUTHOR'S PREFACE

When I first wrote *Fings* I had no idea that it would one day be produced as a musical. In the first instance I saw *Fings* as a straight play, but I can see now that as this it would very likely have not seen the light of day. For it was my first attempt at writing a play of any kind.

It was suggested to me by a friend that I send this first draft to Joan Littlewood at the Theatre Workshop, which I did, and to my amazement she wrote to me saying that she would like to produce the play on her stage. We met and I was introduced to Lionel Bart; and between the three of us we decided to make the play into a musical. We then went to work with the Theatre Workshop Company of actors, who improvised on the character that each was playing, and also, I must admit, on the plot as well until we arrived at the script which is contained in these pages. I now know considerably more about the theatre than I did two years ago.

Frank Norman

POSTSCRIPT

Many of the lyrics in *Fings* owe their inspiration in large part to the improvisations during rehearsals of the members of the Cast. To them I should like to express my gratitude.

Lionel Bart

ACT I
PROLOGUE

A shpieler in a back street in Soho. The front of the stage gives a street effect, street lamp, street door to shpieler, windows, etc. The main set is the shpieler (gambling den) which is in a very bad state of repair. Stage centre is an oval-shaped card table and chairs. Stage right is a tea bar and downstage a little powder room. Behind this, leading up from the street there is a flight of stairs to an unseen first floor. An antiquated telephone stands on a shelf between the tea bar and powder room. Boxing and racing posters are pinned on the walls. At the back of the stage a door leads to a passage. A single light hangs from the ceiling stage centre

The time is V.J. night. The entire company are on stage dancing wildly to a "Hokey-Kokey". A banner is stretched across the stage with the words, "WELCOME HOME FRED" written on it. The company are dressed in various service uniforms. Fred Cochran comes on stage, everyone cheers. Two men bring on another banner inscribed "FROM DARTMOOR". Fred shakes hands all around, walks across the stage arm-in-arm with Lily Smith, picks her up and slings her over his shoulder and goes into the shpieler. The company dance off stage in all directions. A little geezer in a sailor's uniform pinches Sergeant Collins' tin helmet. The stage is deserted for a few seconds; a banner is drawn across stage, reading "TEN YEARS ROLL BY"; the band play a slow beat. Teddy boys and girls wander on in a straggly line, and stare at the audience with contempt. They are dressed in drainpipe trousers, leather jackets, etc. They spread out across the stage

Margaret Where are we going?
Barbara Yeah, where shall we go?
Margaret Let's go to the pictures.
Norman Do me a favour.
Jimmy Don't let's jig about.
Margaret We've been hanging about all night. Let's go and see that rock 'n' roll film.
Norman Wotcha want, a bit of this? (*He jives about*) Rubbish!
Margaret I'd like to see you do better.

Norman jives and sings

Barbara That's nuffink like 'im.
Jimmy Why don't you shut up and stop showing off.
Norman Well, let's face it. How do half these faces get to the top?

As the Teds go off a uniformed copper walks on stage, surreptitiously smoking a cigarette. He stops in the centre of the stage, and notices out of the corner of his eye that Sergeant Collins is coming on from the opposite side. He throws the cigarette away, salutes Collins, Collins steps on the cigarette. A strapping Policewoman enters, also from the right; she has blonde hair and glasses. She goes up to Collins as if to take a pass at him, he cocks a deaf 'un to her and walks in the direction of the strret door of the shpieler. He comes back

G'NIGHT DEARIE (SONG)

Collins Well, 'ere you are boys—on an infamous beat—
Observing the joys of an infamous street—
Attend to your poise, and forget your flat feet—
'Cos 'ere you are boys—
P.C.s 'Ere we are boys.
Collins It's easy ter see when ter make an arrest—
Just take it from me that a bobby knows best
Who's going ter be Her Majesty's guest—
It's easy ter see.
P.C.s It's easy ter see.
Collins And when you're testifying in the law courts
Stop thinking your promotion's very near.
His honour will be prying into your thoughts—
Address the facts unto him loud and clear . . .
P.C.s So's he can hear!
Collins Proceeding in a westerly direction—
P.C.s (Direction)
Collins Saw a lady importuning in the street—
P.C.s (In the street)
Collins After giving her a cursory inspection—
P.C.s (Inspection)
Collins Saying nothing—I continued on my beat.

Exeunt as Betty and Rosey enter from opposite side

Betty ⎱ G'night dearie
Rosey ⎰ G'night honey.
D'you need any company?
D'you feel weary?
You got money?
The best things in life *ain't* free
G'night darling
G'night sailor
D'you feel fit for fun?
G'night dearie
G'night honey
G'night everyone!

Exeunt as Police enter opposite

Collins Pro . . . ceeding with the usual procedure—

P.C.s (Procedure)
Collins In the act, Sir, is where they should be caught—
P.C.s (Should be caught)
Collins But, Your Honour, it's a merry dance they lead yer—
P.C.s (They lead yer)
Collins It was busy, and the time was getting short.

Exeunt. Betty and Rosey return and repeat their chorus, then go off as Police re-enter

Collins Con . . . tinuing the aforesaid line of action—
P.C.s (Of action)
Collins I discovered the defendant in the act.
P.C.s (In the act)
Collins When I booked 'em, they denied a cash transaction—
P.C.s (Transaction)
Collins And informed me they were friends, in point of fact.

The previous "business" with Betty and Rosey repeating their chorus, then go off

Collins 'Pon se . . . eeing that authority is thwarted—
P.C.s (Is thwarted)
Collins By improper recognition of the law—
P.C.s (Of the law)
Collins Well, I only thought it ought ter be reported—
P.C.s (Reported)
Collins How a copper has ter recognize a . . .

Betty and Rosey re-enter and the two choruses are repeated contrapuntally

Betty (*to Policewoman*) That goes for you too, George.

Betty and Rosey go off

P.C. You know wot. I don't think that new bill's going to work.

The Lights fade out

SCENE 1

The Lights go up on the inner set of the shpieler. Fred and Paddy are playing cards, watched by three layabout gamblers. Lily Smith is sweeping the floor It is the early hours of the morning

Fred Cochran is a has-been gangster who is trying to make a come back, at one time he was the governor of the manor but now he is dead skint, and no-one wants to know him except the few slags that go up his shpieler. On Fred's face there are the razor scars of many battles. He is six-foot tall and has very broad shoulders, which are made to look even broader by the wide shoulders of the old, worn-out suit he is wearing. He has a limp and walks with a stick

Lily Smith is about the same age as Fred and has stuck by him through thick and thin, even though he just takes her for granted. Lil has been on the game for over ten years, but, like Fred, she is now past it. Only she knows it and he doesn't

Paddy is an Irishman, and looks it, he always wears a cloth cap, baggy trousers, and an apron. He is very generous and is always good for a touch when he has had a good night, and always lets everyone have things on the slate from his tea bar

Paddy What you got?
Fred You know damn well wot I got—sweet fanny adams.
Betty Nito. (*The cards are hurriedly hidden*)

Sergeant Collins enters by door backstage. A Layabout who has been asleep during the proceedings dives out. Another rushes upstairs

Collins Morning all. There goes young Chataway.
Paddy Well if it isn't old Blue Bottle.
Collins I don't know why he bothers. We've got his photo down at the station.
Paddy Your turn to tiddle, Fred.
Collins Well, well, what's going on here? Tiddlywinks, eh? I hear you've been playing this for three days and nights. You must be pretty tired. Oh well, I'll be seeing you later then, Fred.
Fred Yeah.
Collins Hello, Lil. You're not tiddling this evening.

Collins exits, the cards come out again. Paddy stands up

Paddy Keep your hand on your truncheon.
Fred (*to Paddy*) Where yer goin'?
Paddy What's the point in staying? You're broke.
Fred She's got some. Got any gelt, Lil?
Lil Don't make me laugh.
Fred All right, I'll play yer for 'alf share in the gaff.
Paddy Okay, it's a deal, and just to show there's no hard feelings, you can deal. Show of hands, right?
Fred Right. (*They turn the cards*)
Paddy Well, three lovely ladies.

Fred turns his cards over

Paddy An ace, that's a good start. A deuce and a ten. Well, that's a good night's work. I'm off to get some shut-eye.
Sailor Ain't you gonna give him a chance to win it back?
Paddy Tomorrow, Sailor, there's always tomorrow. Goodnight, all.
Fred I'll play yer the other 'alf.
Lil Never mind the other 'alf. Wot about all that bleedin' three days' washing up in there? Who's going to clean that lot up?
Paddy Give him a cup of tea, Lil. Give it to me new partner, and the best of British luck! Good morning, all.

Paddy exits

Lil Marvellous, ain't it. (*To Gamblers*) And you needn't think you're going to start again.
Fred Do leave off, Lil.
Lil It's enough to drive yer round the bend. Where's me wages coming from?
Fred Ask Paddy, 'e's part owner. Pass me me paper, Lil.

Lil passes the paper

Lil Shift! Nuffink but a load of schnide punters and tuppeny 'apenny whores without a pot between them. Come on, shift. That's all we ever get in this gaff. I said shift.

She puts a stool on the table. The gamblers get out

Lil Cor, it's daylight. 'Ear them sparrows, Fred?
Fred Eh? Oh yeah.

Rosey and Betty come in

Lil Cor, I must be psychic. Now don't you two start laying abaht 'ere. I've got to get the gaff cleared sometime.

Tosher comes in. He is the ponce, wide boy, big mouth, coward, humorist, flash dresser, all in one. Rosey and Betty, his particular "birds", are having a hard time on account of the new "Street Offences Act 1959"

Tosher Wotcher, me old son, and 'ow are we this bright and sunny mornin'?
Fred None the better for seein' you—or am I? Gawd 'elp us, where did yer get that peckham?
Tosher (*fingering his tie*) Wot, the old peckham rye? I fort it was very tasteful.
Rosey 'E nicked it orf a barrer, I saw 'im.
Tosher And 'ow's me little sweet pea this mornin'? 'Allo darlin', 'allo Lil, d'you still love me? Come on, wriggle abaht a bit.
Lil Get out of me way.

Fred D'yer clock the peckham, Lil?

Lil Oh! my good gawd.

Tosher Wot's the matter? Fort yer liked a bit of art and culcher.

Fred Got any gelt on yer, Tosh?

Tosher No mate, I'm skint.

Girls Don't look at us.

Tosher (*trying the telephone*) Never works, that fing. Well, 'ow did it all go last night then?

Betty She nearly got nicked by a policewoman at three o'clock this mornin'.

Rosey Fank gawd she fancied me.

Lil Jolly ain't it?

Betty Fings are getting dead 'ot these days. I fink I'll go straight or somefing.

Tosher Now don't do a silly fing like that. What's going to happen to me? I'd starve, wouldn't I?

Rosey Never mind, darlin', she didn't mean it.

Tosher Well come on then, let's 'ave wot yer got.

Rosey Well we only did a couple of short times all night. The law was all over the place like flies.

Betty Yeah, and on top of that there was a couple of mysteries on the underground selling short times like 'ot cakes.

Rosey At cut price an all, a caser a time.

Tosher Well, come on girls. (*He holds out his hand*)

The girls walk away and discuss how much to give him. They give him a nicker

Do me a favour, this won't even keep me in snout.

Betty Well I can't 'elp it can I, wot wiv all them brasses 'anging out of top floor windows.

Rosey Yeah, them iron hoofs are creepin' in as well.

Lil Them wot?

Fred The proofs.

Lil Oh!

Tosher Excuses, excuses. I always get the same excuses.

Fred You're a real solid gold genuine twenty-two carat ponce, ain't yer?

Tosher I gotta earn a living, ain't I? Get us a cup of splosh, Lil.

Lil Get it yerself, I'm not yer blinking tea boy.

Tosher Well where's that schmock Paddy? Ain't 'e showed up yet?

Lil 'E's only just gorn.

Tosher Nice, ain't it? I fort he worked 'ere.

Lil Fred 'as just given him a 'alf share in the gaff, 'aven't you, Fred?

Tosher Wotever did yer do a fing like that for?

Fred I couldn't odds it. Anyhow, all 'e's got is fifty per cent of nuffing.

Pause

Fred If only I 'ad a few quid ter go ter the races this arternoon. I feel dead lucky—reckon I could earn meself a bomb. I got one of them feelings, you know 'ow I get these feelings, Lil.

Lil Yeah?
Fred Just a few quid.
Tosher It's no use you giving me the old moody, Fred, 'cause I'm skint.
Anyway yer already owe me two quid from free weeks ago.
Fred Don't I always pay yer back?
Tosher Yeah, but it took yer six months last time.
Fred All right, mate, stuff it.
Lil Bloody mean, 'e wouldn't give yer the dirt out of 'is fingernails.
Tosher Oh Fred, yer know me, yer know if I 'ad it you could 'ave it, don't
you?
Betty If you've got it I could do wiv a new pair of nylons.
Tosher Why don't yer belt up?
Fred I can remember the time when yer was well pleased to lend me a few
quid.
Tosher Fred, ain't I always been your best pal?
Fred Not arf, I don't fink.
Tosher 'Aven't I known 'im since the old days when 'e first started up in
the rackets and whose drum did 'e stay in when 'e had it out of the nick
that time? Mine, mine, wasn't it?

The girls agree

Lil You was well paid fer it.
Tosher And who told yer where to find that geezer wot carved you the
first time?
Fred Do me a favour. I'd 'ave found 'im meself without you grassin' 'im.
Wot ever happened to that geezer?
Gambler He's working for French 'Erberts . . .
Lil French Bloody 'Erbert again. Any old how that was years ago.
Fred Yer know, I'm not doing villainy no more. I don't want no bovva. All
I want is to run a nice quiet shpieler, get 'old of a few bob so's I can go
to the races when I feels lucky, like today.
Tosher Well it ain't no use lookin' at me, 'cos I'm skint.
Betty That goes for me too.
Rosey And me.

A man appears in the doorway

Man Is this French Herbert's gaff?
Lil No it ain't.
Man Sorry, my mistake. Could you tell . . .

The Man exits

Lil No we can't. Nice ain't it? (*To Tosher*) Why don't yer go and do a bit
of toutin'?
Tosher What me?
Lil Yeah, you.

Tosher I do the best I can, don't I? They're all going to French 'Erbert's these days.

Lil And do you know why?

Tosher Don't ask me, ask that geezer, 'e's going there.

Lil Well, I'll tell yer why. It's because of bums like you. They come up here to punt and all they see is you and your birds laying abaht and so they shoot down to French 'Erbert's.

Fred Yeah, it don't create a very good impression, yer know, Tosh.

Lil It's your fault for 'aving geezers like 'im work for you—not that I've ever seen 'im doin' any work round 'ere.

Tosher Don't do me any favours, will yer darlin'.

He goes to telephone and dials

Lil (*to Betty*) Do you mind movin' your big feet.

Bett Oh certainly, madam.

Lil sweeps up to make the girls feel uncomfortable

Tosher That you, Sid? Yeah, Tosher. Anyfing buzzin' rahnd your way?

The girls start eating peanuts

No well, I fort I might come over and do meself a bit of good, cause I ain't doin' no good 'ere . . .

Lil Watch my carpet.

Girls Your wot?

Lil I've just swep' it. Did you see that, bloody little sluts!

Tosher Whassay Sid? No, we're dead skint 'ere. Yeah, I try to tell 'im, but 'e don't take no notice of me no more . . . No . . . No . . .

Lil (*to Fred*) Stuck in this gaff mornin', noon and night sweepin' after sluts.

Rosey Doin' wot, doll?

Betty Don't start 'avin' a go at us, Lil.

Tosher No, no-one comes up 'ere no more. No, the birds ain't earning a light, neither.

The girls whisper together

Lil Fred, clear 'im and 'is birds out of 'ere.

Rosey (*whispering*) 'Ear that?

Betty Take no notice, she's 'ad a bad night.

Lil I 'eard that.

Tosher Yeah, well if yer 'ear anyfing for me.

Lil (*to Tosher*) Do you mind keepin' your two birds in line?

Tosher No! French 'Erbert's 'avin' his gaff done out again? Contempery?

Betty and Rosey go into the powder room

Tosher Well, stone me.

Fred Get orf that blower, yer gets on my wick.

Lil You 'eard wot Fred said, get off that blower.

Tosher Do me a favour Lil.
Lil (*to Fred*) Fer two bleedin' pins, I'd belt 'em rahnd the lug'oles.
Tosher Look, Lil, I'm trying to make a little telephone conversation.
Lil So?
Tosher Excuse me a minute, Sid. (*To Lil*) Look I do the best I can, I gave that Rosey a belt round the chops the uvva day and the next fing I knows, Betty 'its me over the 'ead with 'er 'andbag and she only 'as a brick in it wot she keeps for dodgey clients. Sorry about that, Sid.
Lil (*shouting to the girls*) Don't leave yer crepe hair rahnd my basin.
Rosey Moan, moan, moan.
Lil (*to Betty*) Hey, there's other places for doin' that in!
Betty Yea where?
Lil (*to Fred*) You ought to charge for the use of that mirror. In the old days you two wouldn't 'ave reigned five minutes before someone slung a glass of vitriol in your boat.
Rosey And who was it slung some in yours?
Lil I'll swing for 'em! Out of there, come on!
Tosher (*still at telephone*) Nar, nar, girls no bovva. We've enough troubles without you lot 'avin' murders.
Fred (*grabbing Tosher*) Tosher.
Tosher I think I'll 'ave to go now, Sid.
Lil Tosher!
Tosher I'll give yer a buzz before this phone gets cut off. (*He puts the telephone down*) Yeah?
Lil Mind you don't get cut orf.
Tosher Wot's the matter wiv you, you never stop 'avin' a go at us? I fink you must be 'avin' your change of life or somethin' ridiculous like that.
Lil You say that again and I'll kill yer stone dead.
Tosher Fred?
Fred Yeah?
Tosher I fink I'll shoot down the snooker 'all and see if there's anyfing buzzing.
Fred Yeah, you shoot down the snooker 'all and see if there's anyfing buzzing.
Tosher (*to girls*) Yeah, and you two get out and earn. Otherwise I won't be able ter open a faro bank tonight.
Fred An' you find some punters, or we've 'ad it.
Tosher Well, I do the best I can, and there ain't nobody in this world can say I don't.

Tosher exits

Lil You've got to hand it to that Tosher, 'e's about the biggest villain in the entire world.
Betty Comin'?
Rosey Might as well, we ain't doin' no good 'ere.
Lil Betcha a jacks yer don't do a short time between yer.
Rosey Fink you could do better?

Lil Yus, I do.

Rosey Bye, Freddie, see yer later. Don't forget me, lover boy.

Lil Why don't you two crawl back in the 'oles yer came aht of?

Betty and Rosey go out

Fred studies form. He speaks to a Gambler who is asleep.

Fred Wot d' yer fancy for the two fifteen? So do I? Ah, Pretty Girl.

The Gambler snores

The Brass Upstairs walks slowly down to the street

Lil Wot did yer say?

Fred I've been watchin' that nag all season. (*Lil sees the Brass*) Got any gelt in your garters, Lil?

Lil starts to hum.

Fred Lend us a jacks, Lil.

Lil Cor, I'm sick and tired of this gaff! As soon as I get it straight some slag walks in and mucks it up.

Fred Lend us a jacks, Lil.

Lil Where's me wages?

Fred All right, so you've got troubles. Wot about me? Last night was the fird in a row I've done all my gelt.

Lil Yeah, and now you've done yer gaff, ain't yer?

Fred I've got ter bung the law their wack tonight an' all.

Lil Wot?

Fred You saw the look on Collins' face didn't yer? We don't want to be raided again, do we?

Lil And if we do get raided, who 'as to carry the can back?

Fred Do leave orf.

Lil Yer dead ignerant, you are. I don't know why yer bovva wiv it.

Fred Got to make a livin', ain't I?

Lil There's other ways of makin' a livin', there's my bruvver's——

Fred (*cutting in on her*) Your bruvver's barrer. Look, I ain't gonna be no bleedin' barrer-boy at my time of life. Anyway, wotcha screamin' abaht, you're larfin, you are.

Lil Oh I'm laughin' am I?

Fred Yeah, compared to me.

Lil Twenty years on the game and not a penny to show fer it.

Fred Come on Lil, lend us a jacks.

Lil I ain't never 'ad nothin', I ain't. "Lend us a jacks, lend us a jacks." Yer ought to 'ave it put to music and 'ave it as yer signature tune.

Fred Wot abaht that time I took you out on a bender?

Lil When was that?

Fred When I flogged that load of army gear, to Duke Sullivan.

Lil Oh yeah, poor old Duke, 'im wot got topped for doin' in Bert Smith.

Fred Wot about Billy the Burglar! Right tearaway 'e was. Stole 'is Grandma's life savin's and come down 'ere and done 'em in all in one afternoon.

Lil Good old Billy. It was 'im wot brought us together. D'you remember when we first met?

Fred
Lil } In bed. (*Speaking together*)

Lil I fort you 'ad yer gas mask on. Yeah, you was Razor King of the manor . . .

Fred And you was a bright young brass in Dean Street.

Lil Takes yer back, don't it?

They come downstage to the street set

FINGS AIN'T WOT THEY USED T'BE (SONG)

Lil I used to lead a lovely life of Sin. Dough!
　　　　I charged a ton
　　Now it's become an under cover game
　　Who wants to read a postcard in a window
　　　　"Massaging Done"?
　　Somehow the business doesn't seem the same.
　　It's a very different scene.
　　Well you know what I mean.

　　There's toffs wiv toffee noses, and
　　Poofs in coffee 'ouses and
　　Fings ain't wot they used t'be.
　　Short time low priced mysteries
　　Wivout proper histories
　　Fings ain't wot they used t'be.
　　There used to be class
　　Doin' the town,
　　Buying a bit o' vice.
　　And that's when a brass
　　Couldn't go down
　　Under the Union price,
　　Not likely!

Fred Once in golden days of yore
　　Ponces killed a lazy whore
　　Fings ain't wot they used t'be.

　　Cops from universities,
　　Dropsy wot a curse it is!
　　Fings ain't wot they used t'be,
　　Big hoods now are little hoods,
　　Gamblers now do Littlewoods,
　　Fings ain't wot they used t'be.
　　There used to be schools,

> Fahsands of pounds
> Passing across the baize.
> There used to be tools
> Flashing around,
> Oh for the bad old days,
> Remember

Lil How we used to pull for 'em,
I've got news for Wolfenden,
Fings ain't wot they used ter

Fred Did their lot they used ter

Lil
Fred } Fings ain't wot they used t'be.

Fred Lend us a jacks, Lil.

Lil Oh go and ruin yourself.

They go back into the shpieler. Redhot enters on the street. He is wearing a very large overcoat and black hat, and is carrying a large envelope in one hand with the letters "N.A.B." printed on it in large, bold print. In the other hand he is carrying a small hold-all. Redhot has just got out of the nick, for maybe the twentieth time in his life; and the years he has done have left their mark on him. He has to wear the overcoat even in the summer because he has bad blood circulation, and rheumatism, through living in damp prison cells. He has a tendency to talk out of the side of his mouth, a habit formed when working in prison mailbag shops where you are not allowed to talk. He is very nervous and twitches constantly. His only real ambition is to do that one good screwer (burglary) which is going to set him up for life

Redhot (*alone on the stage*) That porridge was lumpy again this morning. Porridge lumpy. . . . Fag end. Used to be that mince. You never see it now though. It's all duff ain't it? (*A Policeman enters and starts walking towards him*) Commissioners, down the Guvnor, chokey, remission. Good behaviour. . . .

Copper 'Allo, Redhot. Let you out again?

Redhot Yes, Sir.

Copper Don't want to see you around 'ere. Plenty of screwers down Bethnal Green y'know. You'll get fourteen years next time.

Redhot I'm goin' down the N.A.B. ain't I?

Copper Oh well, behave yourself.

Redhot Fourteen years. P.D. that is.

Enter the Brass Upstairs with flowers. She drops one. Redhot picks it up

Down the Moor, Up the Ville, Wandsworth . . . Flower ain't it. Yes, don't half pong. . . . Well they let me out y'know, yeah, let me out. . . .

Redhot goes through the door into the shpieler

Fred Stand by your doors!
Lil Redhot! I fort you was in the nick.

Redhot speaks in a prison voice and Fred interprets

Redhot Out for good be'aviour.
Fred ⎫
Lil ⎬ Wot? (*Speaking together*)
Redhot Out for good be'aviour.
Fred 'E says 'e's out for good be'aviour. I see you've still got yer old overcoat on.
Redhot Course I 'ave. Brass monkey wevver, ain't it?
Fred Wot?
Redhot Brass monkey wevver.
Fred 'E says it's brass monkey wevver.
Lil Want a cup of splosh, darling?
Redhot Got anyfing stronger?
Fred Wot?
Redhot Anyfing stronger.
Fred Stronger? No.
Redhot I fort I was goin' to touch yer.
Fred Touch me?
Lil Some 'opes!

Redhot sits down

Fred I spose yer fink you're goin' to lay about 'ere now.
Redhot Well, if yer feel like that, I can always find somewhere else to lay about in.
Fred Yeah, go on, scarper. Get down the National Assistance.
Lil Now then, Fred, 'e's only just done a laggin', you ought to be nice to 'im.
Fred Now who's turned the place into Rowton 'Ouse?

Tosher is heard outside the gaff. Redhot hides in the powder room

Tosher enters

Tosher Come on out, Bloodshot. It's yer old mate, Tosher. I fort you was in the nick.

Redhot, emerging, mumbles to himself

Tosher See you've still got yer old overcoat.
Redhot It's cold ain't it?
Tosher 'E's cold, ain't 'e? 'Ere sit down, Red. Did yer do much chokey?
Redhot Only got nicked once.
Tosher (*handing him tea*) 'Ave a cup of plasma. Got nicked once? Wot for?
Redhot 'Avin' a rabbit in the mail bag shop.
Tosher Rabbit in the mail bag shop? Well, wot 'appened?
Redhot Well, this flash twirl come up to me.

Tosher Flash twirl come up to 'im.
Redhot And said you was talkin'.
Tosher And said 'e was talkin'.
Redhot So I said I wasn't talkin'.
Tosher 'E said 'e wasn't talkin'.
Redhot So 'e said yer was talkin' down the Governor.
Tosher 'E said 'e was . . . down the Governor.
Redhot So we gets down the Governor.
Tosher So we gets down the Governor.
Redhot And the Governor said . . . (*He takes a sip of tea*)
Tosher And the Governor said . . .
Redhot Bleedin' 'orrible ain't it? (*He hands the cup back to Lil*)
Tosher Don't like the tea luv. No sugar. Yeah, well wot 'appened, then?
Redhot The Governor said if 'e said you was talkin' you was talkin'.
Tosher The Governor said 'e was talkin'.
Redhot So I told 'im didn't I?
Tosher Well, wot 'appened in the Death, then?
Redhot Three days bread and water.
Tosher Three days bread and water. Wot a diabolical liberty!
Lil Oh, 'ow yer must 'ave suffered!

Redhot holds his hand out to Tosher for money

Tosher Oh, I fort you 'ad St Vitus Wotsisname.

He gives him fourpence

Lil You're lucky mate.
Redhot Meatface still reigning then?
Fred That grass.
Lil Schnide.
Tosher 'Undredweight of nuffink.
Redhot Big Geezer now though ain't 'e?
All No.
Redhot Can't frighten me, though. The Geezer ain't been born that can
put the frighteners on me.

Three Gamblers come in with Betty and Rosey. Redhot tries to hide

Bill Hi!
George Redhot.
Lou So it is!
Bill Ain't seen yer.
George Couple of months.
Lou Must be.
Mike At least.

The two girls wave to Redhot, then grab him

Tosher Redhot meet Big Betty and Little Rosey, two of the best birds in
the game.

Betty Come on Red, wouldn't you like a little kiss and cuddle then? I can always accommodate you.

Rosey Well, wot's 'e got his overcoat on for in this wevver?

Tosher Cos 'e's cold ain't 'e.

Betty I can remember a time when yer weren't quite so cold, old passion lips.

Rosey No *I* want 'im.

Betty *I* want 'im. . . . 'E's mine.

Redhot breaks free from them and mumbles to Tosher

Tosher (*to the girls*) 'E says 'e wouldn't touch either of yer wiv a barge pole.

The girls turn on Tosher who rushes upstairs. The Brass Upstairs chases him down

Brass Get out of it, what do you think your game is?

Tosher If I come up there I'll do you.

Brass You couldn't *afford* it!!

Tosher My life, don't 'ave anyfing to do wiv birds, Red.

Redhot Birds course I ain't. I'm going back on the old game ain't I.

Lil 'E's off again.

Fred 'Ope you're not reckonin' on takin' over this manor.

Redhot No, there's enough bloody villains around 'ere. I'm gonna graft over the city. . . . (*He mumbles to himself*)

Tosher You wanna watch it over there.

George Gonna work in a Bank, Redhot?

Lil Remember wot 'appened to Donald Hume.

Fred 'Ow much bird 'ave yer done, Red?

Redhot Durin' the war. . . . Wot do yer reckon this, Lil?

He takes a British Rail lavatory mat from under his coat. Lil throws it down in disgust

George Wot's the remission on ninety-five years, Redhot?

Redhot . . . 'Alf a dollar . . . it's a 'ell of a lot.

George If you get nicked again, they'll throw the key away.

Redhot I'm gonna be dead cunnin'.

Fred I ain't seen yer reign fer more than a month, yet.

Lil 'E couldn't give it up. 'E's a proper born tealeaf if ever I saw one.

Tosher You'd better be, 'cos if you get nicked again they ain't even grown the porridge that you're gonna eat.

Redhot Can't eat anyfing else, can I . . .

Bill Do leave off rabbitin' about the nick. It makes me nervous.

Paddy enters wearing a new jacket

Paddy God bless the world. Did anybody think of putting the kettle on?

He starts to clear away the cups

Lil Cor blimey, get the new smother.

Paddy Do you like it? I got it in a shop, it's new.
Tosher Wot's that, genuine shmo'air. . . .
Mike Where d'you knock it off, Paddy?
Paddy No, I paid cash for it, wiv me winnings last night.
Fred You been spendin' my money on clobber. What a diabolical bleedin'
liberty.
Paddy I won it fair didn't I.

Redhot comes up to Paddy

Oh it's Redhot.
Redhot ⎫I fort you was in the nick. (*Speaking together*)
Paddy ⎭
Paddy Who me?
Redhot No me.
Paddy I see you still got your old overcoat.
Redhot Could do wiv a new one.
Paddy Your not very bright this morning are you, Lil, you didn't notice
the bulge in me left hand pocket.
Lil I knew you wouldn't forget me.
Paddy Drop of the old twenty-year-old like yourself. (*He throws cigarettes
to the Gamblers.*) Here fellas spread those among yourselves.
Redhot Got a couple of quid, Paddy?
Paddy I might have known you was coming up with a touch. All right
then, just this once as a coming out present.
Fred What about a reinvestment?

Paddy offers him money

Lil (*giving Fred money*) For Gawd's sake, Fred, what's wrong with mine?
Fred Fanks.
Tosher Like a cup of tea, Red? Get us two teas and two bacon sandwiches,
Pad.
Gamblers An' me, an' me. Make that four.
Fred Eh, Tosh, get on the blower and stick a jacks each way on a 'orse
called Pretty Girl in the two-thirty.
Paddy That thing with three legs.
George That came tenth in a field of nine last week.
Lil Ain't yer done yerself enough damage for one day?
All That's no good. . . .
Fred If I wants to 'ave a bet, I'll 'ave a bet, it ain't your money.
Tosher (*on the telephone*) 'Ullo, is that you, Vernon? . . . This is Tosher,
yeah. . . . Yeah, I'm O.K. 'Ow's the missus? . . . Yeah? Give her one
for me will yer.
Bill Who's ridin' Danny Boy in the free-firty?
Tosher Who's ridin' Danny Boy in the free-firty—'Arry Dot.
Fred Fer Gawd's sake, Tosher, the race'll be over before yer finish rab-
biting.
Tosher (*on the telephone*) Oh yeah, by the way, Vern, Fred wants a jacks
each way on a 'orse called Pretty Girl. It 'asn't got a chance. (*To Fred*)

... 'e says it hasn't got a chance. . . . Yeah that's what I told 'im. . . .
You what? . . . (*To Fred*) 'e says are you feeling lecherous?
Lil That'll be the day.
Fred Look . . .
Tosher All right, Fred. (*On the telephone*) 'E wants it on, Vern. . . . Eh?
all right, all right we'll send the money round right away. I tell you one
fing, Vern, you won't get nowhere while money's your God.
Fred Lou.
Lou Yeah?
Fred Take this cockle round to Vernon's. See it gets there an' all.
Tosher (*on the telephone*) All right, Vern. Cheerio then, don't fall off your
'orse. (*He puts the telephone down*) Vern reckons Pretty Girl ain't got a
chance.
Fred Who asked 'im?
Tosher Fort you'd like to know that's all.
Fred Well I wouldn't.
Tosher Nice, ain't it—all I does is try to 'elp people. . . .

*Betty and Rosey enter in suntops. Betty hits Tosher over the head with her
handbag*

Tosher Now don't you two start. I tell yer wot I'll do I'll ring up Sid and
see if . . .
Lil (*reading a paper*) Wot's your birth sign?
Betty Virgo.
Lil That's funny, so's mine. We got the same fings. Stick to normal
domestic routine and beware of strangers.
Tosher (*on the telephone*) . . . 'Allo, Sid. . . . Oh 'e ain't in. You don't know
where 'e's gone do you? . . . Where, the Oasis? What goes on down
there then? . . . They swim. My life, it ain't natural is it? Well if 'e
comes in tell 'im I was askin' for 'im. . . . Tosher. (*He puts the telephone
down*)
Rosey Ain't it 'ot.
Tosher If it's so 'ot why don'tcha go out and earn, it's just the weather for
it.
Betty Leave us alone, Messina.
Tosher Well, I ain't no millionaire.

*During the first verse and chorus of the following song the Brass Upstairs
comes down into the street, Collins enters from the opposite side of the
street and ogles her across stage*

LAYIN' ABAHT (SONG)

Tosher   Layin' abaht 'ere
Is all very well, dear,
But you'll get a fat rear
From layin' abaht. . . .

Rosey   I do me fair stint.
            I'm coinin' a fair mint,
            So even if you're skint
            I'm layin' abaht . . .
            Restin' me feet.
Company Layin' abaht snoozin'
            Layin' abaht snorin'
Girls   Thinkin' abaht boozin'
Boys   Thinkin' abaht whorin'

Collins goes offstage, Brass goes upstairs

Company Lettin' the thought sink in
            Thinkin' of us thinkin' . . .
            Knowin' we're just blinkin'
            Layin' abaht.
Lil (*scrubbing the floor*)
            Mustn't I be nuts?
            I'm scrubbin' me poor guts
            Out, cleanin' behind sluts
            All layin' abaht . . .
            Airin' their draws
Fred   Used to be big boss,
            Now running a big doss house
            Running a big loss
            Through layin' abaht.
            Cor what a nause.
Company 'Avin' a siesta
            All of us feel sold aht
Fred   Bring on the court jester!
Redhot   Blimey, it's real cold aht!
Company Aht on the streets bashin' . . .
            May bring the old cash in,
            But it ain't arf smashing!
            Layin' abaht.

Collins runs down the stairs into shpieler, struggling into his raincoat. On the street Teds rush jiving across the stage

Tosher Anybody fancy a little game of chance?
Paddy And what are you gonna use for gelt?
Tosher Wot's it to you?
Paddy Well I might win mighten I?
Tosher Well you don't 'ave to play if yer don't want to.
Bill Yeah, that's a point, wot are you going to use?
Tosher You playin'?
Bill No.
Tosher Well shut up. Right, who's playin' . . .?

George Let's see your money first. . . .
Tosher I got my bird's earnin' ain't I?
Fred That's one fing I ain't never been, a ponce.
Lil It's only a rumour.
Tosher Well come on who will, who will?

All place bets

Right no more bets.
Collins I'll have a nicker on the Jack.
Tosher Oh cor blimey, Friday the firteenth.
Paddy I won't bother, you know who's going to win.

The game begins

Rosey Fancy going to the pictures Bet?
Betty We've only just come back.
Rosey Yeah, I know, but I don't want to be around with 'im 'ere.

Collins wins the game

Paddy More money for the Brass Upstairs, Collins.
Tosher All right, any more bets . . .?

All place bets.

Right, no more bets.
Collins I'll have a nicker on the Queen.
Lil When that new Bill goes through you're going to be in dead stook ain't you, Sergeant.
Collins As a matter of fact, I might open a little shpieler of my own one day.
Paddy Yeah it must be very hard on the feet.
Collins It gets monotonous don't it, Fred?
Fred Does it?
Collins Well hows it going? Have you won your gaff back yet or do I have to call on *this* fellow now?
Fred You might as well put it on the Light Programme.
Collins Well come on, Tosher, turn 'em over.
Tosher You sure you wanna play. Have you finished rabbitin'?

Play begins—Collins wins

Tosher If you fell down a sewer yer'd come up smellin' of roses.
Rosey Well I think I'll go to the pictures. Do you know there's a good one down the road all about an 'onest cop, what goes around doin' good turns?
Collins Yes and if you want to do any more good turns you'd better watch your mouth.
Paddy Don't be like that, Seamus, I'm just going to put the kettle on, will you join us for a cup of tea?
Gamblers An' me . . . an' me.
Rosey Do we get one, Paddy?

Tosher Don't give 'em anyfing. Once yer give 'em one fing they wants another.

Paddy If I wants to give 'em something I'll give it to 'em and I shan't ask your permission before I do.

Tosher I hope they knocks yer for the gelt then.

Betty Oh come on, Rosey, its too 'ot for tea anyway. I'll treat you to a nice ice cream.

Rosey What I could do with is one of them long knickerbocker glories. . . .

Betty and Rosey go out

Tosher Now where do they get the money for that? Couple of fly customers them two birds of mine.

Collins brings out wallet to put his money away.

Paddy Devil takes care of his own.

Lil How much do they pay them in the force these days, Fred?

George Well they get a big boot allowance.

Collins Well I'm trying to save up for a rainy day you know. Well so long, Fred, but not too long. (*To Tosher*) Watch it.

Collins goes out

Tosher Give us a kiss!

Rosey enters downstage, on the street

Rosey And cherries and cream you know and all that fizz, and ice to keep you cold.

Betty Rosey you must 'ave a cast-iron stomach.

Rosey You got to 'ave, in our business.

They see Collins and run

Redhot There ain't 'alf a draft in 'ere, cuts right acrossed yer, don't it?

Tosher Why don't you walk from Edinburgh to London?

Redhot If I did you'd still be rabbitin' when I got back. I tell you what though . . . (*He comes downstage and sings*):

WHERE IT'S HOT (SONG)

> If only I could be
> Somewhere across the sea
> Where's it's 'ot . . .
> Really 'ot.
> Where breezes never blow.
> Bejeezus I could show
> Wot I've got—really got.
> I'd like to take a pleasure boat off
> To somewhere where the sweat can float off

Perhaps I'd take me overcoat off . . .
Somewhere. . . .
Where it's 'ot.

Oh, set me on a beach,
And let me peel a peach
Where it's 'ot. . . . Boilin' 'ot.
Me little bathing suit
Would show the little cute
Beauty spot. . . .
On me bot.
Before I go and lose me grip, please
Shanghai me on a cruiser ship please
I wanner go and do the strip-tease
Somewhere. . . . Where it's 'ot
Somewhere where's it's 'ot!!

Company Olé!
Tosher (*at the card table*) Anymore for anymore. Come on who will.
Right, no more bets.
Lil I'll 'ave a 'alf dollar on the Queen.

Lil puts down a bet.

Tosher You gorn deaf, I said no more bets.
Lil Who the 'ell are you talkin' to?
Gamblers Yeah. . . . (*He mutters*)
Fred (*quietly*) Rap up!
George Don't have a go at me, I was stickin' up for. . . .
Fred (*suddenly shouting and brandishing his stick*) All right that's enough.
Get the 'ell out of 'ere. The lot of er. Go on, scram, vamoose, vanish.
And you. Look at this place, it's supposed to be a shpieler, it looks more
like a bleedin' doss 'ouse. (*Finding another sleeping Layabout*) You 'eard
what I said. It's about time they realized who they're talking to. Who'd
they think they're talkin' to a big geezer like me.

The Layabouts and Gamblers flee, Tosher follows

Redhot Talking to 'im a big geezer like that.
Fred Still am a big geezer.
Lil You still are.
Redhot Big geezer before they was born, 'e was. . . .
Lil Course 'e was.
Fred That's right, Razor King of the Manor.
Lil (*proudly*) Yeah, 'e's got press cuttings to prove it. 'E's been in the papers
you know, Red.
Redhot You been in the papers, Fred? 'As he been in the papers?
Paddy Sure, 'aven't you seen them, Red?
Fred Give 'im a butcher's Lil.

Lil gets a press cuttings' book

Lil Which one shall I start at?

Fred About nineteen-firty-two, when I was a real tearaway.

Lil (*reading*) " 'Ooligan terrorises maiden ladies."

Fred They weren't no maidens.

Lil "Fred Cochran taken into custody. The notorious Razor King was in bed when the police raided his Mayfair maisonette." He lived in Mayfair y'know.

Fred Yeah, not for long though, that was a dead dodgey manor to live on that was, in those days.

Paddy Still is, Fred, still is.

Lil "At the local police station, he was charged with slashin' free members of a rival gang. Asked by the police if he had anyfing to say, he replied, 'They done me first so I done 'em back.' How long are these gangsters to be allowed to terrorise peaceful citizens? This paper is offering a reward" . . . a reward.

Fred Don't matter wot the paper said. They didn't do nuffink. In actual fact, that reporter was my publicity Agent.

Lil That's not a good likeness is it?

Paddy Terrible, terrible.

Lil Never liked that one, makes him look like a real villain don't it?

Paddy Look at this one. (*He laughs*) Fred Cochran after he was sentenced to four years' penal servitude.

Fred Wot's so funny about that?

Paddy Yeah, what's so funny about that?

Lil 'Ere, Fred, look at this one. Where was that?

Fred That was down on the French Riviera.

Lil 'Ere, Fred, look at my 'air there.

Fred Cor, look at me there. Yeah, and look at me now. Damn near fifty.

Lil Fred, you ain't.

Fred Well I'm forty-five and that's damn near fifty.

Paddy Prime of life Fred.

Fred Yeah, if you're on the up and up. If only I could get me 'ands on a bit of gelt. I'd do this stinkin' gaff up. I'd show that French 'Erbert. If I can't run a better shpieler than 'im, I'd shoot meself.

Paddy He's got the backing of the big geezers, Fred.

Fred So 'e gets a bit of protection from that grass Meatface Heiman, he finks he's the guntz and he ain't.

Lil Who, Meatface?

Fred Yeah, 'e ain't worth nothin' and never will be.

Lil Never heard of 'im in the old days.

Fred Yeah, that's the old days, Lil. That's me there. You and your new smother. I had six suits a week and two for Sundays. And that's me bowlin' up in me Rolls-Royce.

The Lights go out

Lil Who did that?

Paddy Anyone got a bob for the meter?

Fred Anyfing in the till?

Paddy No.
Redhot 'Ere, try this tiddleywink.
Paddy Why didn't I think of that?

The Lights come on

It works, I'll remember that Red.
Lil I never noticed that before. That crack in the ceilin'. Did you notice
it . . . ?

THE CEILING'S COMIN' DAHN (SONG)

Lil   The ceiling's coming dahn,
          And we never even knew.
          We've been too busy doing what we
          Fort we ought to do.
          While we wander through this life
          Of our'n,
          The ceiling's coming dahn.
Paddy The meter's sprung a leak.
          Shall I leave the kettle on?
          We keeps on putting shillings in,
          But all the gas has gone.
          Wot a thing t'be an old antique!
          The meter's sprung a leak. . . .
Lil   And the ceiling's coming dahn
          Ter fink I could have been
          An housewife in
          A bungalow wivout no stairs.
          The blokes I could 'ave wed
          Are old or dead.
          I stuck around for Fred, but where's
          The ring?
          I wears one in me dreams,
          And I sees meself in white.
          A pretty little posy
          In me 'and I'm holding tight.
          I looks down and shatters all me dreams—
          Me skirts have split their seams,
Paddy And the meter's sprung a leak,
All   And the ceiling's coming dahn.

Redhot goes—Tosher rushes in brandishing a newspaper

Tosher It won, it came 'ome, Fred, you're made. It came 'ome.
Fred You sure you didn't make a mistake. You know you can't read.
Tosher I didn't 'ave to, some geezer told me.
Fred For once in yer life you didn't make a ricket. It won all right, look.
Lil Darlin', now you can buy me a nice birfday present.

Fred 'T ain't yer birfday.

Lil Well. I didn't get nuffink when it was me birfday.

Paddy You've about a monkey to come.

Fred Do you know what I'm gonna do? I'm gonna 'ave this gaff done out.

Lil Fred you're not.

Fred I am. No more slag.

Lil Fred, I've seen a lovely dress.

Fred No more riff raff layin' abaht.

Lil It's a lovely dress, Fred.

Fred We're gonna run a real smooth shpieler.

Lil It's a real smooth smother.

Fred Paddy, ring that geezer who's got the builder's yard round the corner and tell 'im I've got work for 'im to do.

Lil Can I 'ave it then, Fred?

Fred Wot?

Lil The dress.

Fred Yeah, yeah, 'ave 'alf a dozen.

Lil Oh I love you.

Paddy (*on the telephone*) That you, George? . . . No I don't want to borrow anything. Fred reckons he wants you to come round and do the gaff up. (*To Fred*) When do you want him to come?

Fred Right now.

Paddy Fred said right now.

Fred And tell him I don't want no excuses. If he ain't round right away, I'll be round for him wiv a meataxe.

Paddy Fred said——

There is a clatter on the stairs. Horace Seaton rushes through the door followed by George the Builder. Horace is a queer interior decorator. He is dressed in a pair of tight-fitting white trousers, green jacket, purple pullover and bow-tie. He walks and behaves mincingly

Oh you 'eard what he said.

Horace I did.

Fred Wots 'e?

George That's my mate, 'Orace. 'E works wiv me. 'E's a genius.

They all watch Seaton walk round.

Fred 'Ere, Mister—Miss. D'er fink you can do somethin' wiv it?

Horace Well I know what you *could* do wiv it.

Fred Wot?

Horace Oh well never mind dear, we'll do a lovely job for you. First lets see. George, those chairs, *out*. Oh yes, now I'll tell you what I see right down there—a jardiniere. Relieve the bleakness. And—Oh yes, now that table.

Paddy Well I thought of a nice bit of formica. . . .

Horace Formica!—firewood, dear.

Fred Ain't nobody going to move that table I'll tell yer. And up there I want one of them chandelissy fings.
Horace Oh no, not all that cut glass and gilt.
Fred Don't worry about the gilt, I'm loaded.
Horace Oh no, you don't understand. I thought a Rise and Fall.
Tosher Wot, in the room?
Horace Do you *mind*. No, no. Anodised Satin brass. Very pretty. Now lets see. Oh Coca Cola. . . . Charming. I know, a Paul Klee and right across 'ere.
Fred Red Plush.
Horace No, no, Bamboo, dear.
Fred Red Plush.
Horace Red plush is just too camp, ain't it?
Fred Now don't mess about. Do you know French 'Erbert's gaff?
Horace French Herbert. No, I'm afraid I've not had that pleasure.
Fred Well I want it better than 'im see. More leary.
Horace Leary?
Fred Yeah, double leary.
Horace Oh no. You got to be tasteful. Contemporary. Nowadays everything's modern.

CONTEMPERY (SONG)

Horace Sooner or later ev'ryone has got to go
            Contempery. . . .
All Contempery.
            Soon as the paint is on the wall then you will know
            Contempery. . . .
Horace Contempery.
            In my house I've got rubber plants and cactuses
            Believe me, sir, I preaches what I practices
            For very small expenditure, you too can be
            Contempery.
Mystery They're changing the style at Buckingham Palace
Horace Oliver Messel is full of malice.
            They've painted the wall that faces the yard
Girls In pillar-box red to match the guard. . . .
Horace And Alice!
All Eyes right!
Fred Sooner or later ev'ryone has got to go
            Contempery . . .
All Contempery
Horace Look at the lamp-posts up and down the Rotten Row
            Contempery. . . .
All Contempery
Horace There's coffee tables one foot high to trap your knees
Girls Descending to the level of the Japanese
Tosher Who's gonna be the geisha girl who brings the tea?
All Contempery.

Horace	Colours! But not the same two twice
	Colours! And never mind the price
All	Colours. . . . You must 'ave colours,
Horace	'Cos you'll agree, sir, that colours are nice.
George	Have you ever caught your builder in a gay mood
	Wiv a paintbrush in his hand?
Horace	He'll do anything you ask him, within reason
	If he thinks you understand.
	There's a little spark just waiting to be kindled
	You've been swindled up till now
All	Come on. . . . 'Ave a splurge. . . .
	And fire his urge and he will show you how.
	And sooner or later ev'ryone has got to go
All	Contempery. . . .
	Contempery.
Horace	Over the mantlepiece we'll 'ave a Pickerso!
	Contempery. . . .
All	Contempery
Horace	So take away your Coca-Cola calendars
	You'll be surprised what a little talent does!
	Here's to the G-plan furnitchewer
Tosher	Here's to the hole by Henry Moore. . . .
George	Here's to the stripes on ev'ry door
	You will see!
All	Con-tem-per-y!!

Painters bring on their gear. Horace follows them about, with George the Builder behind him

Horace (*to audience*) It's going to be lovely.

CURTAIN

ACT II

Scene 1

Late afternoon the same day. The gaff has been done up in modern fashion, "contempery". The Curtain *goes up on a Boozing Party. George, the builder, and Paddy are dancing a jig. The rest are singing, applauding or just boozing. As the jig ends*

Fred Drinks all round. Pass round the booze, Paddy.

The bottle goes round. George and Horace bring in a modern table

Tosher You want to mind you don't get stinkin', guv. You gotta be double shrewd tonight.
Fred Don't worry about a fing. I'm makin' a comeback.
Tosher Fred Cochran will return! What's that—(*pointing at table*)—a banjo? 'Ere, give us your number, Fred.
Paddy Yeah, come on, Fred, your party piece.
Fred No.
Tosher Go on, Fred. 'Orace ain't 'eard it.
Fred Wrap up, then!
Paddy One voice.
Fred 'Orace!
Horace Yes.
Fred Park your ass and pin back yer lug 'oles. Ow does it start?
Paddy I was sitting in a boozer.

COCHRAN WILL RETURN (MONOLOGUE)

Fred I was sittin' in a boozer back in Nineteen Twenty-nine
　　　I'd never done no villainy then, plumbin' was me line.
　　　When in walks this 'ere copper, and he books me china, Jim,
　　　So I sticks one on his hooter—makes a bloody mess of him.

　　　From there on I'm a tearaway—I'm living in the nick—
　　　I has a coupla bundles, and I cottons on dead quick—
　　　I'm doin' the odd screwin'—and I'm nimble up a pipe—
　　　And, by the way, by this time I'd acquired me virgin stripe. . . .
　　　(It's a pretty one, en it?)

　　　Well, in Nineteen Thirty-two I leaves the smalltime to the mugs.
　　　I has me last night's kip in prison beds wiv prison bugs.
　　　I goes a bit legitimate—I changes my abode—
　　　I buys a one armed bandit arcade dahn the Mile End Road.

All Mile End Road.

Fred I gets a reputation as an 'ardcase double 'ard,
And a little team ter follow me—all wanted up the yard.
But there's one ambitious geezer, and 'e's 'andy wiv a spanner—
'E tries ter run my business—so I runs him off the manor. . . .
(He left his mark though.)
It's Nineteen Thirty-seven, and the East End is my place—
I moves in on the West End—I meets Lil, and we go case.
I opens up five shpielers—everybody else goes broke—
It looks like I'm about to be the guv'nor of "The Smoke".
One foggy night I'm coming aht me gaff in Berwick Street
When I hears the pitter patter of a dozen tiny feet—
I looks around ter clock the sound—it's Jack the Prince's mob—
Between the six of 'em they did a thorough facial job. . . .
(Like a railway line, en it?)

Horace Very nasty.

Fred When they lets me aht of 'orsepiddle I visits Jack the Prince—
They must have stitched him up bad cos we've never seen 'im since.
I commandeers the race-tracks—and I straightens out the law—
I'm doing well—and then some slag called 'Itler starts a war!

On top of all this bovva, me accountant goes right bent
And lumbers me wiv income tax!—that's when me Rolls Royce went.
So it's dahn to flogging clothing-coupons—one fer 'alf a note—
Then a lump of flyin' shrapnel comes and cops me up the froat.
(I don't usually show this one . . . But it's a good job that 'Itler
done *hisself* in . . .)

When the final all-clear sounded, back in nineteen forty-five
I may have been boracic lint, but I was still alive,
I tried to track down all me mates wot used ter be me mob
And I finds that half the bastards 'ave secured another job.

It's this 'ere schnide called Meatface—who imagines 'e's the king.
And 'e's only pulling all the fiddles Cochran used ter swing!
And tho my Lil is quite prepared to go outside and earn
I've sent a note to Meatface sayin' . . . "Cochran will return"! . . .

All Fred Cochran will return!

Applause. Healths are drunk. Paddy and George re-commence their jig

Fred Tosher! I'm goin' round to collect me winnin's.
Tosher Right, guv.
Fred You get on the blower and start raking in the customers, right?
Tosher Right.
Fred Strictly class, mind yer.
Tosher Strictly class.
Fred (*to the room in general*) Quiet, you slag! Can't 'ear meself fink.
Tosher Fred says knock it off.

Horace has gone offstage, he now returns, holding a cactus plant

Horace Is it all right for us to press on, Mr. C?
Fred (*to Tosher*) Start wiv Honourable Percy Fortesque.
Tosher 'Orrible Percy Fortesque.
Fred There's all me old contacts in me press cuttin's book, Paddy!
Paddy Fred?
Fred Press cuttin's! An' I want 'em all back again! Right? All me old
muckers!
Paddy ⎫
Tosher ⎬ Right. (*Speaking together*)
Fred Horace, take yer finger out.
Horace Spoil sport.
Fred This gaff's openin' t'night. (*Going*) Drinks all round, Paddy, on the
'ouse.
All Farewell, Fred.

Fred exits

Horace (*to Paddy*) These'll have to be watered every morning, from the
bottom up.
Paddy (*looking at cuttings*) Oh sure, sure.
Horace And you'll have to watch the castoroils, give 'em every care and
attention. We don't want our prickles wilting, do we?
Tosher Very dangerous them prickles. Wouldn't 'ave 'em in the 'ouse.
Ric (*a Gambler*) All right to have a game of cards in 'ere now, Tosh?
Tosher Er, course.
Mike (*another Gambler*) What do we play on?
Tosher All right for them to play cards on your banjo, Horace?
Horace (*angrily, to Tosher*) You'll have to go, you know. No taste.

The Mobile comes on

Tosher Wot's that? (*He shakes the Mobile*)
Horace Don't meddle. I've been up all night with that.
Tosher Must 'ave been very uncomfortable.
Paddy Tosh, for God's sake, get on with what Fred says.
Tosher Wot was that then?
Paddy Phoning them geezers!
Tosher Oh yeah, the 'Orrible Perce.
Horace 'Onourable dear.
Paddy 'Onourable, 'orrible, what's the difference? (*He thumbs through the
cuttings*)
Paddy Here he is. "Lady Cockleech's tirara was stolen last night while she
was giving a cocktail party. The honourable Percy Fortesque was the
chief guest."
Tosher Don't say where 'e lives though, do it?
Paddy Yeah, Beul Hill Ponds.

Horace Bewley, dear.

Tosher goes to the telephone

Paddy No, Beul Hill.

Horace Pronounced Bewley.

Tosher Wrap up! Is that Beaul Hill Ponds? Can I 'ave a little rabbit with the Duke please.

Paddy Tosher, don't muck about.

Tosher Just for a giggle, like. Ho! 'e hain't in residence. And to whom do I 'ave the pleasure? It's 'is butler, oh marvellous. Well, wot about the 'Orrible Perce then? Oh 'e's just down for the Regatta. Righteo, I'll 'ang on then. (*Aside*) Lovely place for a screwing.

Paddy (*indicating Seaton*) Tosher! Look, how long are you going to be fiddling around there, Horace?

Horace Rome wasn't built in a day, dear.

Paddy Yeah, but that was a bigger gaff.

Tosher I can just 'ear 'is footsteps comin' along them old baronial passages. Can't yer see all those photos on the wall? Where's our Redhot?

Ric Where's that drink Fred said?

Paddy There's none left.

Ric Well, I'm dyin' of thirst, ain't I.

Paddy So am I, but there isn't any.

Mike Make it splosh then.

Lou An' me.

Neville (*another Gambler*) An' me.

Tosher 'Orace'll take one wiv us, won't you 'Orace.

Horace Ta very much, two lumps. None for George.

Gamblers Stick, twist, bust.

Tosher Wrap up, 'e's 'ere.

The Gamblers go on murmuring

Paddy Quiet, the lot of you. If Tosh lands a bit of muzel for tonight, we'll all be laughing, won't we.

Everybody listens to the telephone call

Tosher (*on the telephone*) 'Allo 'Orrible, bet you don't know who this is? This is Fred Cochran's butler. You remember Big Fred, the King of Soho? ... Yeah, well why I actually rung you was Big Fred's 'aving a grand openin' night tonight an' 'e thought you might like to come along and do in a few fifties, like you did in the old days. (*To the shpieler*) 'E said, 'e'd be glad to come, fishy ain't it.

Mike Very!

Paddy Marvellous.

Horace Bobo Fortesque, I've heard of him.

Tosher Very fishy. (*He rings off*) Who's next then?

He and Paddy consult the book.

Ric (*his feet on the table*) Where's that splosh then?

Horace Do you mind dear—feet!
Mike Why don't you jump into some lake or somefing?
Horace (*astonished at himself*) Why don't you wrap up!

He goes offstage

Paddy Try this one—Sir Sidney Pane.
Tosher Give us it, 'ere.
Paddy What's the use when you can't read?
Tosher I can read numbers, can't I?
Paddy I'll make the tea. (*At the bar, shouting*) Horace, how am I sup-
posed to get behind there? I mean, look at the place, it's chaotic.

Horace brings the bamboo on

Horace Over here, George. Do you mind for a minute, all of you.

He arranges the bamboo in the centre of the room, disturbing the Gamblers.
We hear the mutter of their game as they go and play upstage at the old table.

Paddy (*from the tea bar, showing a little teapot*) Hey, Horace, what the
hell's this?
Horace A teapot dear. Very pretty.
Paddy Where's my *brown* teapot?
Tosher (*on the telephone*) It was on the table, and she threw it out. 'E
ain't in.
Paddy Did she?
Horace I don't think this bamboo's going to work. (*To George*) Fancy
anyone being so kinkey about a brown teapot.

He goes off

Tosher Who shall I try now?
Paddy I don't know. You've got the book, haven't you? (*He recovers it*)
Fred'll go bloody mad if you put your dabs all over it like that.
Tosher Do leave orf.
Paddy Who's this, some old colonel. . . .
Tosher No that's old Pinhead, that is. Guvnor of Wandsworth. What's
Fred got 'im in 'ere for?
Paddy Or this one, Maharajah of Serapire.
Tosher 'E got trampled to deaf by elephants.

Mike drags the table centre with Ric

Mike Excuse me, Paddy.
Ric Can't see the cards over there.
Tosher I'll tell you wot, Paddy.
Paddy What!
Tosher I'll use me own pernishetive.

Paddy You do that. Now look here you lot. Fred's got class coming in here tonight.

Mike (*proceeding to Horace's table*) Can you play cards on that fing?

Paddy No!

Tosher (*on the telephone again*) Is that Chinese Charlie's gaff?.. No, his drum, his kip, his lumber gaff. Wot's the matter wiv yer, don't yer speak English? . . . Oh, only Chinese. No, look, 'e's a punter. . . . Oh, 'e was a punter.

All take their hats off

Paddy God rest his soul.

Tosher Fourteen years. P.D. My life, 'e'll never serve it, who's that speakin' then? Wozzo? Not Wozzo Newman? It's Wozzo! This is yer old mate, Tosher. Never recognized yer.

Paddy Will he come?

Tosher (*on the telephone*) No, look, well don't go, Woz. . . . Yeah, Fred's openin' a new gaff t'night.

Paddy Don't tell him it's a new gaff, he's bound to tumble it's the old 'un.

Tosher (*on the telephone*) I'm told to tell yer it's the same gaff wot's been done out. Eh? . . . You remember the last time. . . . Well it wasn't my fault, Woz. I was always your best mate, wasn't I, Woz? . . . Well, shut yer mouth too, then. (*He slams the telephone down*) My life!

Horace minces on, with large flower in his hand

Paddy Horace, you look like a whore at a Christening.

Horace Who moved my table?

Paddy Fred said to keep the old one.

Horace And spoil the whole of my design?

Paddy How can they play cards on that?

Horace It's a very pretty shape.

Paddy So are you. So was my brown teapot.

Tosher (*rubbing his sleeve*) Look at that, paint all over me new smovver.

Horace (*suddenly in a rage, and almost throwing the flower at Tosher*) George! Take the table away! Burn it. Chop it up! Do what you like with it. I don't want to hear no more. An' nobody *needed* to get paint on their smother, I'm sure.

Horace walks downstage in disgust. Lil comes through the door at the back of the shpieler. She is dressed up in a cocktail dress, which is brown with lorge white polka dots all over it. Like the shpieler she has undergone a complete transformation and looks very posh.

Lil Oh, it's nice, very pretty. (*Sees chairs*) Oh, look! Pity about the old table, though.

Horace stops in his tracks. Paddy signals George to exit with new table. George exits

Lil (*to Horace*) Did you do all this dear?
Horace All except the table.
Lil I think it's smashin'.
Horace Well, if I could have carried my idea through. . . . Stay there dear!
Don't move, please. Here. (*He collects Paddy*) No, just look, from here,
the polka dots and that striped wall, together.
Lil Do I go?
Horace (*to Paddy*) See, you're fab!
Lil Eh?
Horace Fabulous.
Lil From now on. . . .

POLKA DOTS (SONG)

Lil   From now on there's gonna be . . .
Lots n' lots
Of polka dots
Wiv chunky gold accessories.
Horace . . . Accessories
Lil   Rows n' rows
Of hanging clo'es.
You'll wonder who my dresser is.
Horace . . . Dresser is
Lil   Shorty nightie. . . .
Horace Eye Tiddly Eyetie
Lil   Smothered in forget me nots
Both   Life will be
A symphony,
Wiv lots of polka dots.
Tosher (*speaking*) She's gorn potty.
Lil (*speaking*) I can just see meself now—like one of them ladies in house
and garden dressed immaculate and servin' tea and crumpets off a
trolley . . . and what else . . . what else.
(*Singing*) In our gaff we'll have to have
Lots of gin
And whisky in
A shiny cocktail cabinet.
Horace Cabinet
Lil   I shall choose
Who drinks the booze—
We'll have no old lags grabbin' it.
Horace Grabbin' it.
Lil   In our posh drum
Paddy Pass round the slosh chum!
Lil   We'll entertain big shots.
Wot a treat—
The three piece suite,

Lil
Horace } Wiv lots of polka dots.

Lil (*speaking*) Yes. And on the curtains too . . . 'cept we'll 'ave plain lace
ones underneath cos' that's more respectable. I tell you, we're gonna go
short of nuffink. . . . nuffink.

(*Singing*) This 'ere Miss's shopping list'll read
   On the firm
   A four quid perm,
   Together wiv a manicure.

Horace Manicure.
Lil   Colour rinse
   Wiv silver tints—
   And let the old man panic—you're

Horace Panic—You're . . .
Lil   Still his Judy—
   He'll pull a moody—
   Then, darling in you trots—
   Real refined,
   And he'll be blind
   Wiv love, and lots
   And lots, and lots,

Lil
Horace } And lots of polka dots.

Horace Well that's my lot.
Lil Who's going to clear up this mess then?
Paddy If we all put our backs into it it'll be lovely.
Lil Well I'm not puttin' my back into it in this new dress.
Horace Nor me, in this drag, dear.
Lil 'Ere, 'ave you got one of those fings that beats as it sweeps as it
cleans?
Horace I don't know what I'll be asked for next. Now don't forget, dear,
that's your wall.
Lil No I won't forget dear. Ta ta, darlin'. Look at them bums.

*Horace goes out. Redhot sneaks through the door backstage, carrying a
smart-looking suitcase, colourful labels stuck all over it*

Gamblers Hi, Lil.
Lil They're still 'ere.
Tosher Yeah.
Lil Did Fred say or did 'e not say that there was to be no more slag, no
more layabouts, no more ponces?
Tosher Are you bein' personal!
Lil Yeah, go on get 'em out of 'ere, the lot of 'em.
Tosher Wot abaht your mate Redhot?
Lil Redhot an' all.
Tosher There 'e is.
Lil Hello, darlin'.

Redhot I just done a screwer, I ain't half got a load of gear.

Fred enters

Lil Wot. . . . 'Ere, Fred, I thought this gaff was goin' to be respectable for once in its life.
Fred Wot . . .
Lil Well look 'e's just done a screwer!
Fred Eh! (*To the Gamblers*) Come on, scarper. Get 'em out, Tosh.
Tosher All right, boys, see yer later. (*He winks at the Gamblers and sees them off*)
Fred Well, come on, let's 'ave a butchers.
Lil Your promises ain't worf nuffing.

Fred goes over to the suitcase, takes a very flash looking tartan smoking jacket out of it

Fred 'Ere what d'yer reckon this for me openin' night?

He tries the coat on

Redhot Don't keep turnin' it over, it won't be worf a light.
Paddy (*finding a silver cup*) Bit big for an egg, ain't it?
Tosher My life, they won't 'alf 'ave the dead needle when they find that missin'. Wot's it say on there?
Paddy The Blue Hill Ponds Angling Club.
Lil 'Ow much do you want for the smother, Red?
Redshot I'll take a tenner.
Tosher He'll take a tenner.
Lil Tenner, cor blimey, take it off, Fred, it's rubbish. 'Alf a quid.
Redhot Sackville Road that is.
Tosher 'E says it's Savile Row.
Lil More like Club Row.
Redhot Ain't it all right, I goes out risking my liberty and I gets robbed.
Tosher Yer wanna take it, Red, yer won't get that much down Moishe Greenman's.
Redhot All right, but I wants cash.
Tosher 'E says 'e wants cash.

Lil has found wallet in the jacket and pays Redhot with money from it

Betty and Rosey enter

Rosey It's pouring with rain. Look at my 'air set, Tosh, it's ruined. What 'ave you got there?
Tosher Nuffing for you, darlin'.
Rosey We never get anyfing nice.
Redhot Nar then, hands off.
Lil Cor dear, fings is still the same round 'ere. Tosh and his birds, Red'ot still going out screwin'. I thought you was going to turn this lot in. Cor fings ain't changed a bit 'ave they?

Rosey (*picking up a piece of lace*) Look, Bet, ain't it luvverly?
Betty Wot is it?
Rosey It'd do lovely for a poufe.
Betty For a wot?
Rosey One of them fings yer sit on. I'm goin' to keep it for me bottom drawer. Can I 'ave it, Red?
Redhot No yer can't.
Paddy Go on, give it to her. It's not worth a light. Go on, Rosey, have it.
Betty Tosh, look wot I've found.

She puts a fur round her shoulders

Lil Fred, look she's only got a fur smother.
Redhot Mink.

He grabs it and starts to sneeze. Everybody sneezes as imaginary moths fly out

Tosher (*stamping on it*) Kill it, kill it. . . .
Lil Oh, Fred, look. A silver fruit bowl, fruit an' all. I always fancied one of them. (*She puts it on the table. It has red apples in it*)
Betty Did yer go scrumpin' while yer went screwin', Red?
Redhot I didn't 'ave no time did I. Swep the lot in didn't I? 'Ere, come on, who's been nickin' all my gear?
Paddy Now as if anybody would do a terrible thing like that.
Tosher Nito.

Redhot sits on the case, covering it with his overcoat. Lil squats on the silver cup

Collins enters

All 'Allo, Serg. . . .
Collins So where's the suitcase?
Redhot Wot suitcase? You gorn potty or somefing. I ain't got no suitcase 'ave I? (*Collins noses around*) I only got out of the nick this mornin', didn't I?
Tosher You'll be back this afternoon if you don't belt up.
Redhot Do yer fink I'd walk about with a suitcase in broad daylight and get meself done for sus.

Collins finds the fur.

Tosher (*gesticulating*) Yeah, it walked right down there right round there and out there, never said a word.
Paddy Must have been a stray.

Collins finds suitcase

Collins All right, open it.
Redhot It ain't mine

Redhot cannot open it

Collins Don't bother. Fred, can I see you outside a minute?
Fred (*quickly*) Get that gear out of here.

Fred and Collins exit the gaff and stand on the shpieler's doorstep on to street

Tosher 'Ere, stuff that up yer garter.
Paddy He's in a right mood ain't he?
Lil Yeah, there's somefing buzzin' all right. Fine fing when the law are supposed to be 'aving better relations with the public.
Tosher Get it out of 'ere.
Redhot Can I put it behind your bar, Paddy?
Paddy No you can't.
Rosey I 'ope 'e didn't see me poufe.
Betty Oh shut up about your poufe.
Tosher (*sarcastically to Redhot*) I'd stay there if I was you. Don't matter that it looks dead sus does it?
Lil 'E's 'avin' a right old bunny with Fred.
Tosher What do you reckon 'e wants Fred for?
Lil 'Is wack. What else does 'e come round 'ere for?

Redhot goes out

Paddy There's something in the air and I don't like it.

They all sit and wait for Fred to return

Collins (*outside the shpieler door*) So things are dead dodgey all round.
Fred Wot yer worried abaht, Meatface or yer job?
Collins My whack.
Fred I bung yer when I got it and when I ain't you 'ave ter wait.
Collins Yeah, well right now you've got it.
Fred No, right now I'm dead skint. I threw it all into 'avin' the gaff done up.
Collins Really? Well, I've just left Meatface.
Fred Oh yeah.
Collins Yes, just a moment ago, and he's not so keen on this opening night of yours.
Fred So wot abaht it?
Collins So if you don't look out you're on your own. I'm not sticking my neck out for peanuts.
Fred Consider yerself knocked.
Collins I hope you've still got it in you, Fred. Ten years ago you were the best. Five years ago you could have made a comeback, but not now . . .?
Fred We'll see.
Collins Yes, we'll have to see. Looks like rain don't it?
Fred Yeah, don't it?

Collins goes. Redhot comes downstairs

All Where is it?

Redhot I gave it to the Brass Upstairs.

Betty That slag. There won't be nuffing left in it.

Redhot Yeah.

Paddy You might as well have given it to Collins.

Redhot It's better than bein' swagged down the nick. 'As 'e gorn?

Lil Gawd knows.

Fred enters

Tosher It's Fred, it's all right.

All Well?

Fred Wot's the matter wiv everybody.

Paddy What did he want?

Fred 'Is wack.

Paddy Oh that ol' thing.

Lil Well, did yer give it 'im?

Fred No, I bunged 'im a load of the old moody and stuck 'im in the land of promise. Well, wot are you all layin' abaht for? This gaff's got to be ready for tonight.

The telephone rings

Tosher I ain't 'eard that phone ring for months.

Fred Well go on answer it someone.

Tosher Yeah, of course. (*He goes to the telephone*) 'Allo. Oh 'allo, Sid. It's Sid. I fort you was dahn the Oasis observin' the bird life.

Redhot Observin' the bird life.

Tosher Wot? Yeah, that's right. 'E's just been in 'ere too.

Redhot 'E's just been in 'ere.

Tosher Wot? No, I don't believe it.

All Wot?

Tosher No. 'Ow many of them? Cor, it just goes ter show, don't it?

Fred Wot goes ter show?

Tosher Just a minute, Sid. (*To Fred*) Sid reckons Collins just raided the. boozer round the corner and nicked a load of the 'ounds.

All No.

Lil So 'e just came for 'is wack did he?

Paddy That's the first time Collins has nicked anybody.

Tosher Shut up a minute. (*Into the telephone*) Who got nicked then, Sid? . . . Well, I never did reckon that geezer. . . . A dozen of them. . . . You don't say. . . . Any of Meatface Heiman's mob? . . . No, definitely none of Meatface's gang. . . . French 'Erbert's 'ounds? No, all lone wolves.

Redhot Lone wolves.

Tosher Small timers, 'asbeens? Oh, yer reckon Meatface is at the back of it.

Fred 'Ow does 'e reckon that?

Tosher Fred says 'ow d'yer reckon that? Well 'e says the only time Collins gets busy is when someone is puttin' the bung in, and 'e reckons it must

be Meatface. Thanks, Sid. You comin' up 'ere tonight? . . . Wot d'you
mean, we ain't openin' . . .? Well we ain't scared of 'im or Meatface
either, are you, Fred? Eh? Oh! They found Liver Lips wiv 'is ears cut
off this morning? Oh yeah, see yer. Don't get run over. Dodgey ain't it?

They hold the mood

A Busker in tattered clothes rushes into the street

Busker (*staccato, to a drum accompaniment*)
    Who ran away with a blind man's hat? MEATFACE.
    Who does a murder just like that? MEATFACE.
    When there's a fight his day's well made.
    He's a proper villain with a razor blade.
    Meatface. . . . I'm warning you . . . and you.

He points to the audience, then runs off. After a pause—

Lil Got a drink, Paddy?
Betty Give us a drop, Lil.
Tosher Don't drink that stuff, it'll rot your drawers.

A burst of sinister music, to be repeated in the "Carve Up" song later

Betty Fred. Wot time'll fings start opening up?
Fred Give us a swig of that poison, Paddy.

"Carve Up" music

Betty Fred, wot time d'you fink fings'll start openin' up?
All (*nervously*) Fred, what time. . . . What's going to——
Lil (*cutting in*) Shut up the lot of you, 'e's got a lot on his mind.
Redhot Lot on me mind.
Fred Load of slag. Meatface wouldn't stand for 'em for two seconds.
    You've got to hand it to 'im, 'e's a right shrewd nut.

"Carve Up" music

Tosher ⎫ Yus.   ⎫
Paddy ⎬ You said it. ⎬ (*Speaking together*)
Bett ⎭ 'E is an' all. ⎭
Fred You fink I'm worried about 'im?
Tosher No, you don't 'ave to worry about 'im, guvnor.
Fred I said I wasn't worried abaht 'im.
Tosher Well, if you ain't worried about 'im, we ain't. Anyway 'e can't do
    nuffink to yer.
Fred If 'e comes round 'ere, 'e'd better start worrying about what I'm
    goin' to do to 'im.

"Carve Up" music

Fred (*shouts*) Lil!
Lil Yeah.

Fred Wot's the time?
Lil Don't know.
Paddy Late.
Betty Smashin' ain't it?
Tosher Wot?
Betty Well, it's all 'appenin' ain't it?
Fred Tosher! Shoot rahnd the manor and put the word about. Fred
Cochran's openin' tonight.

The telephone rings. All go except Paddy, Lil, Fred and Rosey

Paddy (*on the telephone*) It's Meatface.
Fred Ask 'im what he wants.
Paddy (*on the telephone*) Fred says, what do you want? . . . You!

"Carve Up" music

Fred (*on the telephone*) 'Allo, Meatface. 'Ow yer keepin'? . . . Oh, I'm
glad to 'ear you're still on yer feet. . . . Yeah, I'm openin' tonight. . . .
Yeah, I've had the place done out a bit contemporary like. . . . Eh?
Look 'ere, I'm openin' tonight, and if you want to stop me you'd better
come round 'ere and bloody-well try. . . . All right ain't it, you can't do
nuffing these days wivout somebody tryin' to stick 'is 'ooter in it.

Fred slams the telephone down

Busker rushes on to the street again

Busker (*as before*)
Who let his old girl die in pain? MEATFACE, MEATFACE.
Put her down the lav' and pulled the chain. MEATFACE, MEAT-
FACE.
When there's a fight his day's well made
He's a proper villain with a razor blade.
Meatface. . . . (*To the audience*) I told you about that geezer before ..
And I wasn't joking neither. . . .

He exits as before

Lil (*to Fred*) Now you've done it, ain't yer?
Fred Rosey go 'ome. Lil, I'm gonna get myself a 'aircut and shave. If the
class come before I get back, keep 'em entertained.
Lil Fred! I'm comin' wiv yer.
Fred Why?

He goes.

Lil You 'eard what Fred said, clear out.
Rosey Yeah, all right.
Lil Find somewhere else ter lay about in.

Rosey You fink I ain't got no 'ome? Well, I 'ave.
Lil Well I know the sort of 'ome you'll end up in.
Rosey Why? My old lady's still on the game.
Lil So's my grandmother.

Lil goes out

WHERE DO LITTLE BIRDS GO? (SONG)

Rosey Where do little birds go to
In the winter time?
There'll be blizzards and snow too,
In the winter time.
And the thought of it horrifies me so.
Where do, where do,
Where do little birds go?

What will become of all those little larks
Now there is no more nesting in the parks?

Mummy used to go out and catch the early worm.
She'd not told them about the big and burly worm.
He can only be pulled by some old crow.
For their breakfast
Where do little birds go?

What'll become of all those wee tom tits?
Who's gonna save the soppy little twits?

When they're wondering why they
Took the westward flight.
Want to snuggle inside their
Childhood nest tonight.
When those wintry winds (Shakespeare) doth blow.
Where do, where do,
Where do little birds go?

*The Lights fade in shpieler. Teds come on downstage on the street, Fred
from the opposite side*

Norman Excuse me, Guv, you're Mr. Cochran ain't yer?
Fred (*looking offstage*) So?
Norman I fort it was you.
Fred So?
Norman My old man told me about you, Mr. Cochran.
Fred So what?
Norman One of these days I'll be where you are. And if you want any fing
done——

Fred Yeah?

Fred goes offstage

Norman You know who that was? Fred Cochran! One of *the* biggest villains on the manor. Recognized me an' all.

All the Teds jeer at him.

Norman Shut your face, peasants.
A Ted Any more orders, Dad?
Norman Yeah, I'll tell you.

BIG TIME (SONG)

Norman When the big times come
I'm gonna have me some
I'm gonna do the fings
My Daddy never done.
I'm gonna get rich quick,
And you're a lucky chick
If you're around when I'm
Big Time!

Let 'em all get lost!
I won't be double-crossed.
I know the fings I want
I know the price they cost
I'm gonna get my share
While I've still got my hair
I'm on the upward climb . . .
Big Time!

No more Woolworth raids
And showing off wiv blades
Trips to Notting Hill
For punches-up wiv spades
Let all the other yobs
Have tupp'ny ha'p'ny jobs
I'm hearing Big Ben chime. . . .
Big Time!

Big guys are cool
Just like an icicle.
I'm gonna fix this chain
Back on the bicycle
I'm gonna use my wits
Instead of just my mitts
So long! Small-time crime. . . .
Hullo! Big Time!

How I get up there. . . .
Well, that's my own affair.
Cos I can buy my friends
When I've got cash to spare
I'm gonna fill the till
I'm gonna top the bill
In this 'ere pantomime. . . .
Big Time!

When the big times come
I'm gonna have me some
I'm gonna do the fings
My Daddy never done
I'm gonna get rich quick
And you're a lucky chick
If you're upon the scene when I'm
Big time!
I'm gonna be *so* big!

*During this song stage fills up, Teds on street, rest of cast except for Fred,
in shpieler, all of them executing an increasingly frenzied rock 'n' roll
rhythm. The song over, Norman and Teds drape themselves downstage.
Fred enters shpieler, clad in Tartan dinner jacket while cast in still
dancing*

Fred (*entering the shpieler*) Wot the 'ell's going on 'ere?

Fred enters the gaff

Betty We're 'avin' a little rock ain't we?
Fred Wot are all those slags doing in 'ere?
Tosher Well if they comes in to punt they comes in to punt.
Fred The 'Orrible Perce showed up yet?
Tosher No not yet.
Fred 'E said 'e was comin' didn't 'e?
Tosher Yeah, said 'e was, said 'e was.

*Percy and Myrtle enter on the street, quizzed by the Teds: Percy in tails, silk
scarf, top hat; Myrtle in cocktail dress with a very peculiar hat. They sing*

THINGS AREN'T WHAT THEY USED TO BE (REPRISE)

Percy   This place used to be a rave,
         Now it's one foot in the grave,
         Things aren't what they used to be.
Myrtle I try getting sweeter
         Competing with Lolita,
         But things aren't what they used to be.
Percy   There used to be Noël—

Terribly tired—
Where are his friends today?
They're all on the doël
Drably attired.
How can a guy go gay on
Moss Bros?

Myrtle Clothes don't make a man, dear,
But you do what you can, dear.

Percy But things aren't what they used ter,
Time's right for a booster.

Together Things aren't what they used to be.

Paddy (*in shpieler*) You don't arf look smart in your new smother, Fred.

Redhot Yeah, yer got a bargain there yer did.

Fred You tryin' to be funny?

Redhot No, Fred.

Paddy The trouble with you is that you're never happy unless you're havin' a go at someone.

Percy and Myrtle knock at door to the street. Tosher answers it

Tosher Who is it?

Percy The Honourable Percy Fortesque.

Tosher Wot's the password?

Percy Black Maria.

Tosher No, don't muck about. Wot's the password?

Percy My dear fellow, it's been Black Maria since 1936.

Tosher No, it's 'Ope Springs Eternal.

Percy Very well, Hope Springs Eternal.

Tosher lets them in.

Tosher Introducin' the 'Orrible Percy Fortesque—and bird.

Percy Hallo, Hallo, Hallo. . . . Oh, Freddie, it must be centuries.

Fred 'Allo, Perce, wot 'ave yer been doin' wiv yerself?

Percy Oh one thing and another you know, getting involved, involved. Oh, Myrtle, I want you to meet a frightfully good friend of mine, Freddie Cochran.

Myrtle (*her voice is extremely affected*) Cochran, oh I say.

Fred 'Ow do yer do, 'ow are yer keepin'.

Percy No relation to C. B., dear.

Myrtle Oh I'm frightfully well, thank you. (*Looking around*) Oh, isn't it all awfully quaint here!

Betty and Rosey giggle

Tosher Pack it in.

Fred Tosher, take the 'Orrible's 'at and stick.

Tosher Nice to see yer, Guv. Lovely bit of gear this.

Percy I say Freddie, you do look chic.

Fred Yeah, I've just 'ad the gaff done up a bit contempery. . . .

Percy No, I mean the jacket . . . extraordinary thing, the old man had one exactly the same but some bounder broke in last night and stole a whole lot of things including a jacket.

Fred Er, yeah, it just goes ter show don't it, yer can't leave anyfing layin' about these days.

Percy Oh well, never mind. (*To Betty*) Haven't I seen you somewhere before? Come on let's have a little game of faro shall we.

Fred All right, Perce. Come on you lot, make some room. Well, Perce, wot's the limit.

Myrtle Oh, he's ever so reckless you know.

Tosher Hi hi. (*He sits next to Myrtle*)

Myrtle (*waving*) Hi.

Tosher 'Ow's it goin' then?

Myrtle Oh I'm frightfully well thank you.

Tosher Oh that's nice ain't it.

Myrtle Yes.

Tosher D'you do the town very often, darlin'?

Myrtle I'm sorry, what did you say?

Tosher I said do yer come up the West End very often?

Myrtle Oh no, not much these days, you see the Bentley is so expensive to run. . . .

Percy Myrtle for God's sake, there's nowhere to park the bloody thing.

Myrtle Oh that isn't true, darling, naughty.

Girls Naughty, naughty, naughty.

Myrtle (*to Tosher*) He thinks he can talk to me any way he likes now that we're engaged.

Tosher Do me a favour, darling. I mean you must 'ave been 'aving it off with ol' Perce for some time now.

Percy I say old chap, do you have to talk to Myrtle like that?

Tosher Sorry, Guv, no offence.

Myrtle Oh it doesn't matter.

Myrtle laughs, the Punters all stare at her

Myrtle (*waving to them*) Hallo.

Mike Speakin' to me?

Myrtle Oh aren't they lovely darling? So unaffected.

Tosher They're a bunch of schnides.

Myrtle What did you call them?

Tosher Schnides.

Myrtle What a lovely word. What does it mean?

Tosher (*whispering in her ear*) Naughty.

Betty (*to Rosey*) If she don't get out of 'ere I'll scratch 'er eyes out.

Rosey The old bag, she must be thirty if she's a day. You'd fink she'd be past it.

Myrtle Are they friends of yours?

Tosher Oh yeah, they're my birds. That's Big Betty and Little Rosey.

Myrtle Birds? What a lovely, word darling. Oh, what a lovely tie.

Tosher Wot, you mean the old peckham?

Myrtle The tie. Oh yes, I think it's very gay.

Tosher You can 'ave it if yer like, darlin'.
Fred Wrap up can't you, Tosher.
Tosher I was only 'avin' a little rabbit wiv the damsel.
Fred Yeah, I know all about your little rabbits.
Betty So do we. If you don't leave off we'll do you.
Rosey That goes for me, too.
Tosher I don't know. I can't say nuffink around 'ere wivvout people
gettin' the wrong idea.
Percy Oh, I say, I've lost again, Myrtle.
Myrtle Darling, how awful.
Percy Do you know, Freddie, it's uncanny you sitting there in that
jacket. I keep thinking it's the old man.
Redhot I'll getcha one for 'alf a quid.
Fred 'Ere, Tosh, have a decko dahn the street and see if there's any class
arrivin', they might be findin' it a bit difficult to park.
Tosher Yeah, all right, Fred.
Percy What did I tell you, there's nowhere to park, the place is full of
bloody Vespas and Cadillacs.

The telephone rings

Paddy (*on the telephone*) Wrap up, will you. I can't hear a thing.
Percy It's a free country isn't it, or thereabouts.
Paddy (*on the telephone*) Speak up can't you, there's a hell of a row going
on, we've got a cabaret going on. . . . Oh Hallo, Meatface. Meatface.

At this the Gamblers, except Percy and Myrtle, rush out

Fred Ask 'im 'ow 'e wants it, tools or a straightener.
Percy My dear, that sounds bloody obscene.
Paddy (*on the telephone*) How do you want it?

He indicates to Fred it is to be tools and puts the telephone down

Tosher comes in, hesitates

Fred Come on, Tosher, sit in on the game.
Tosher Eh?
Fred Sit in on the game.
Tosher Fort that's what yer said.
Fred You too, Paddy.
Tosher Reckon you can do 'im, Fred?
Paddy He's a right hard case.
Betty Wot's the time, Tosh?
Tosher Late.
Betty Shall we go out, Rose?
Rosey Ooh! No! Not tonight, Bet.
Betty Why not?
Rosey Not with all them villains around.
Betty Oh shut up, you make me sick.

Fred (*nodding to Tosher to follow him, leaves the table*) Er, you got any snout on you, Tosh? (*Quietly*) Lend us your tool. (*He takes a razor from Tosher*)

Percy (*while Fred is talking*) Do you have any gaspers, Myrtle?

Myrtle No, darling, you had the last one in the taxi.

Fred Well, come on who's going to have a bet?

Myrtle May I, poodles?

Percy Go on then, you'll only lose the rest.

Tosher (*to girls*) Don't 'ang abaht, get out and earn. I gotta live ain't I?

Rosey I don't see why.

Percy One up to the girls!

Tosher Wot's the matter wiv you, mug, you lookin' for bovva?

Percy Where's your sense of humour?

Tosher If yer don't watch it I'll punch you on the end of the 'ooter.

Fred (*to Tosher*) Wrap up.

Percy What a bore. . . .

Tosher Wot did you say?

Myrtle Darling, you've offended him. Naughty.

Betty Goodnight, Fred, best of luck.

Fred Fancy goin' case tonight, darlin'?

Betty No thanks, I'm trying ter give it up.

Fred How about my little sweet pea?

Rosey Me neither. I'm savin' my cherry till I get married.

Betty and Rosey go out

Percy Have you got any gaspers, Freddie? I'm dying for a smoke.

Fred Got any snout, Pad?

Paddy All right to flog those you got the other night?

Fred Yeah.

Percy Have you got any Benson and Hedges?

Paddy What do you think this is, the Savoy?

Percy Hardly, dear boy.

Paddy All I've got is a nice line in American snout.

Percy Oh God, Colonial manure. Oh well, they'll jolly well have to do won't they?

Paddy That'll be a caser.

Percy What did you say?

Paddy Five shillings.

Percy All right, you'll get it. Anyone would think it was a bloody fortune.

Paddy (*suddenly realizing*) He's skint.

Tosher Oh no.

Paddy Oh yes. Yeah, well, I'm just going out to light a candle.

Tosher Well I fink I'll go out and stick some Stars of David on a few Methodist churches.

Paddy and Tosher go. The atmosphere grows tenser, but Percy and Myrtle don't notice

Percy Oh is everyone going? What a shame.

Fred 'Ave you got wot yer owe the 'ouse?

Percy Oh, Freddie, of course I haven't, you know me. I can give you a cheque if you like to try your luck.

Man at Door Meatface says, are you comin' out or is he comin' in?

Fred I'll 'ave it outside.

Fred gets up and goes out on to the street. The Teds enter down-stage, silently follow him and stand watching. Fred goes off

Percy (*in shpieler*) Oh I say they've all gone.

Myrtle What a frightfully dreary place, darling.

Percy It used to be such fun in the old days.

Myrtle Well, maybe it did, but it isn't now.

Percy I know, let's go round to see Charles. . . . Oh no, he's dead. Well we always used to go to Bobbie's, but they put her away. I know, let's go round to Noels, he's a bit of a bore, but he's good for a free drink.

Myrtle What a good idea, darling.

They get up. Percy looks for his hat and stick

Percy Oh God, they've taken them too, they must be hard up.

There is the sudden clatter of a fight offstage. They go out on to the street. Myrtle screams and rushes off. Tosher, Paddy, Betty and Rosey come on, look anxiously offstage and then go off. The Teds are left alone

CARVE UP (SONG)

Norman ⎫ Carve up!
Teds ⎰ There's just been a
           Carve up!
           We've just seen a
           Carve up!
           In-between a
           Kickin' and a slashin',
           And a nickin' and a bashin'
           Wot a carve up!

           Knives an' all!
           Some carve up!
           Wot a ball—
           This carve up!
           It was all
           Much quicker than we reckoned—
           It was over in a second—
           There was
           Blood all over the place—
           Blood all over his face—

Wot a medical case—
From ear to ear is twenty-seven stitches
Wot a carve up!
There's just been a
Carve up!
We've just seen a
Carve up!
We're not green—
(It's only our complexion)
Wot a great
Carve up!!
  Great carve-up!

CURTAIN

SCENE 2

Later the same evening. Paddy and Tosher are sitting at the table. The following scene is acted at a much slower tempo

Paddy What a carve up, what a bloody carve up. Never saw anything like it in all me life. Did you?

Tosher Never, never.

Paddy If he'd have nodded his head it would have fallen off into the gutter.

Tosher Don't keep on abaht it.

Paddy Did you see his teeth that time when his mouth was closed?

Tosher Yeah, all right, all right.

Paddy I knew it. It was there on the wall for all to see.

Tosher All right, don't keep on abaht it. Get us a cup of splosh.

Paddy There's none. Anybody with an eye in his head could have told him.

Tosher Don't talk abaht eyes.

Paddy I knew it.

Tosher Yeah, all right. I'll tell you one fing. There's bound to be a comeback.

Paddy All right so there's a comeback, so we knew nothing about nothing.

Tosher Yeah, but when the screams come I don't wanna be around.

Paddy What's the matter wiv you? There's always been bother around here but no one's ever got nicked on this manor with old Collins reigning.

Lil enters

Tosher Yeah! But is 'e reigning now? Soon as my birds show I'm gonna 'ave it away on a number eight bus to Old Ford, I'll tell yer.

Lil Wot are yer talkin' abaht?

Tosher Oh 'allo Lil.

Lil Was that Fred out there?

Paddy Well, er yeah. . . . I suppose so.

Lil Where is 'e?

Paddy Well . . . don't know.

Lil Did yer see wot 'appened?

Paddy Well there was a bit of a carve up, wasn't there.

Lil Did yer see wot 'appened?

Tosher Well, no, not exactly, yer see . . .

Lil (*scornfull*) Yeah, good old Tosher, Fred can always rely on you when 'e's in trouble. Well, what 'appened?

Paddy Well, nothing much, only Fred done the living daylights out of about half of Meatface Heiman's mob. He'd have done Meatface an' all if he was there.

Lil Did 'e get cut?

Paddy Well, yes, he got himself a little stripe, but he's got so many another one won't make any difference.

Lil An' where was you two when all this was 'appening?

Tosher Yeah, well, by the time I got there like it was all over, and Meatface and his boys were 'avin' it away down the street. I reckon they saw me comin'.

Lil I bet.

Tosher Wot do yer mean by that?

Lil Do yer really want me to tell you?

Tosher Yeah. . . .

Lil Well, I'll tell yer, I reckon yer the lowest fing on this earth. You got a yeller streak dahn yer back as big as Balham bloody 'Igh Street.

Paddy Now, Lil, don't get in a panic.

Tosher Go on, let 'er tell me. . .

Paddy Look, this is getting us nowhere fast. What we've got to do is to have a good story for the law when they shows.

Collins enters

Tosher Listen, mate, I ain't worried about the——oh gawd blimey.

Collins We had a nice bit of fun and games last night, didn't we?

Tosher Oh yeah, we 'ad a lovely opening night.

Collins All right, let's have it, what happened?

Tosher What do yer mean, what 'appened? We 'ad a good opening night.

Collins Don't give me any of the old moody. Where's Fred?

Tosher Well I suppose 'e's at 'ome 'aving a lay in.

Collins Don't have a go at me. Now I don't mind a bit of bother but when it comes to blades and on my manor, well that's a bit strong, isn't it?

He sits down. There is a long pause

Paddy It's all right, Lil. Sergeant Collins isn't staying long, are you, Sarge?

Collins It all depends, doesn't it?

There is another long pause

Tosher Would yer like a cup of tea, Guv.

Paddy (*to Tosher*) We ain't got any.

Tosher Look, this is ridiculous, Collins, ridiculous. I mean you never used ter mind if there was a bit of bovva every now and then just as long as none of the public got 'urt. I mean, didn't yer 'ave an arrangement with Fred . . .

Collins That was in the old days, things have changed, and in any case what I get off Fred these days doesn't hardly keep me in snout. Now Meatface, that's a different cup of tea, he looks after me double well.

Lil That's all you fink abaht, your wack. I'd like to see yer come unstuck one of these days, Mr Policeman.

Collins Now don't be like that, Lil. I've got to make a living, ain't I?

Lil Livin'? I don't know wot you're doin' alive at all.

Redhot comes in through the door

Tosher Nito, nito, nito.

Collins Come in, Red.

Redhot I ain't got no suitcase.

Collins Did I ask you if you had a suitcase?

Redhot No.

Collins Well wait until you're asked.

Redhot Wot do yer want me for then?

Collins Did I say I wanted you? Did I, Tosh?

Tosher No.

Collins It comes to something when two old friends like Redhot and I can't have a cosy little chat together now, doesn't it?

Redhot I fort you didn't like me.

Collins Oh, I'm very fond of you, Red. Where's Fred?

Redhot looks at the others. Tosher nods his head slowly from side to side

Collins What's the matter, Tosh?

Tosher Bit of a stiff neck, that's all, must be the wevver.

Redhot Can I fall out, Sarge?

Collins No you can't.

Paddy and Lil have been talking in whispers

Collins Something on your mind, Paddy?

Paddy Well, I was thinking, it's no use to us all 'angin' around here is it. I'll tell you what happened, Sergeant.

Tosher Paddy!

Paddy What's the odds? I know the Sergeant couldn't care less, could you, Sergeant?

Collins No, Paddy.

Paddy Well last night, two geezers come up here and started a load of bother.

Collins Who were they, Paddy?

Paddy Well, that's the bit I don't know about. They were a couple of square swedes. I ain't ever seen 'em before.

Tosher Me neither.

Redhot Nor me.

Lil Don't look at me, I wasn't 'ere.

Collins Well?

Paddy Well the next thing I know is that Fred offers 'em outside and he follows them and on my life that's all I know.

Tosher And me.

Redhot And me.

Lil I told you I wasn't 'ere.

Collins Well how come when I was in the hospital just now I saw three of Meatface's terrors laid flat on their backs with bandages all round their heads?

Paddy Oh! the traffic in the West End is terrible.

Tosher Terrible yeah. Well it just goes ter show you don't it?

Collins Is that all? (*Suddenly shouting*) All right then, you, you and you, you're nicked.

Tosher Wot charge?

Collins Withholding evidence, it'll do until I can think of something else.

Paddy This is the way he repays us for all the help we have just given him.

Collins If you think I believe your story, you're potty.

Tosher I like that. After all we done for yer we deserve a job in the force.

Collins You deserve a sock on the jaw.

Tosher Look, you can't take me dahn the nick. I'll get done for being an incorrigible idiot or somefing, I got form against me.

Rosey and Betty come in

I can't get nicked again, can I?

Rosey 'Allo, Sergeant Collins, I didn't see you standin' there.

Collins Hallo, Rosey. The boys have just been telling me that you know where Fred is.

Rosey Yes, I know where 'e is.

Tosher No, don't tell 'im.

Collins Watch it, Tosher.

Rosey 'E's round at our gaff. We took 'im there after 'e had that bother with them geezers last night. 'E didn't want to go to 'ospital 'cos 'e was afraid of gettin' nicked. 'E's very comfortable.

Collins That's the truth, isn't it, Rosey?

Betty Course it's the truth. Rosey don't tell lies.

Tosher Never, never.

Collins It had better be. You know what'll happen, Rosey, don't you, Rosey? It's awfully stuffy in there at this time of year. (*To Tosher*) Wipe that smile of your face or I'll nick you for obscenity.

Collins goes out

Tosher Wot, me!

Redhot I ain't stayin' 'ere, it's knee deep in grass.

Paddy What did you want to go and do a thing like that for?
Lil Nuffing but a pair of grassers.
Betty Leave 'er alone, she don't know nuffing, she was with me all night.
Rosey Yeah, don't 'ave a go at me, I don't know where Fred is.
Lil Don't anyone know where 'e is?
All No.
Betty Anyway, we fairly pulled the wool over old Collins's eyes, didn't we.
Tosher Yeah, I gotta 'and it to you two birds, you did a good job there.
Paddy I'd give you a cup of tea if we had any.
Tosher But I 'ate to fink wot the antecedents of this will be when Collins finds out that you gave 'im a load of the old moody.
Rosey Well, you'll worry about that for us dear, won't you? After all you're the Boss.
Betty Smashin' night though wasn't it? I thought the claret'd never stop pourin' off Fred's boat.
Tosher Do leave off, you make my flesh creep. 'Ere I've got a good idea, let's go down to the Oasis and see Sid and 'ave a little sunbathe.
Lil That's right, Tosher, you go and find yerself a new gaff, just when Fred needs yer.
Tosher I never said nuffing abaht a new gaff, all I said was I was goin' down the Oasis for a sunbathe. Can I 'elp it if 'e does 'imself every time? I've always been 'is best mate, ain't I?
Betty Yes.
Tosher Well, tell 'er then.
Betty 'E's always been his best mate.
Tosher (*to the girls*) Are you comin'?
Betty Yeah.
Rosey No.
Tosher (*to Rosey*) Well stay here then.

Tosher and Betty go

Lil Ain't there no loyalty left in this world?
Rosey Never mind, Lil. I'm not goin' wiv them. Shall I stay and keep you company, luv?

Fred comes slowly down the stairs, a big patch of plaster on his face. Paddy waves Rosey out of the shpieler

Lil Fred!
Paddy You feeling better now then, Fred?
Lil Where you been?
Fred Upstairs in the Brass's gaff.
Lil Whyever did you go up there?
Fred Cos it's the last place the law 'ud fink of lookin'.
Paddy Old Collins ain't 'arf been looking for you.
Fred (*very grimly*) 'E won't have far ter look. Give us the shooter, Paddy.
Paddy What do you want that for?

Fred I said give us the shooter.

Lil (*frightened*) Wotcha gonna do, Fred?

Paddy gets gun from behind counter and gives it reluctantly to Fred

Fred I'm gonna give that Meatface a tuning up, 'e'll be sorry 'e 'ad a go at me.

Lil But yer can't go out like that, Fred.

Fred Get the place ready for openin', Lil.

Lil Wot are you gonna do?

Fred I'm gonna kill 'im stone dead.

Collins enters

Collins Hello, Fred.

Fred backs against wall and pulls the gun

Fred Collins, I've just about had enough of you . . .

Paddy (*shouting*) Don't shoot a copper, you'll be topped!

Suddenly the tension drops. Fred lowers his gun

Collins You bloody fool. I *feel sick.*

Paddy So do I. Here, this'll put the colour back in your cheeks. I'm sorry it's Scotch.

Collins What a day, all this and Ponders End.

Paddy Eh?

Collins Ponders End.

Paddy Oh you want to get that seen to.

Collins No, no, I've been transferred to it.

Paddy Oh we're going to miss you.

Collins Meatface. I reckon Meatface put the mix in with the Governor. I'd do that Meatface if I could lay my hands on him.

Paddy You and whose Army!

Collins If he ever comes to Ponders End. I don't know what I am going to do.

Paddy You could open a shpieler in Connemara—oh it doesn't appeal to you.

But the idea of a shpieler does appeal to Collins

Collins I don't even know the Governor at Ponders End. I'll have to get all new contacts.

Paddy God love yer.

Collins I've a good mind to resign from the Force.

Paddy Have you seen your feet lately? Ah, you wouldn't know how to be anything else but a bogey.

Collins Well, I'll tell you something.

During the song Tealeaves and Brass enter and dress Collins in brightly coloured clothes for shpieler

COP A BIT OF PRIDE (SONG)

Collins Now, if I had a shpieler,
Complete with a dealer,
Complete with a tea bar as well,
I'd love it, I'd love ter
Say I'm me own guvner,
Respected by my clientele.
Tho' you may not believe what I say,
I dream of that wonderful day. . . .

When every villain in the manor is me china,
Instead of thinkin' of me only as a snide.
When all the tealeaves and the brass
Are pleased ter see me when I pass
And every sneakin' little grass
Is finished creepin' up . . . I ask
Yer, is it worth it havin' everybody hate me
Becos of what I may be getting on the side?

I want to be the chap who drops,
Instead of me (who only cops),
I want to cop a bit of pride.

I want you to see . . . whatever I look . . .
I'm eager to be an honest crook!

Betty Who's heard of coppers ever stopping being coppers
Who knows a bogey that is not a thorough snide?
If you can tell me where's there one.
Who wouldn't sell his only son
Well then—so help me—I'm a nun
My clientel can take a run
But don't you worry boys that's never gonna happen,
Because I know you're being taken for a ride.

Collins I want to be the one who drops,
Instead of me who only cops,
I want to cop a bit of pride.

Betty He's ever so good
He's ever so pure
Send him to Brighton for a cure!

Chorus When every villain in the manor is your china,
Instead of thinkin' of yer only as a snide,
When all the tealeaves and the brass
Are pleased to see yer when yer pass
And every sneakin' little grass
Has done his dirty rotten business
Is it worth it having everybody hate yer,
Because of what yer may be getting on the side?

Collins I want to be the one that drops,
          Instead of me (who only cops),
Chorus He wants to cop a bit of pride!
Collins (*speaking*) Honest!

Fred and Collins start talking. The Cast mask them from the audience. When seen again, Collins, complete with eyeshade, is at Fred's place at a gambling table

Collins Honest! Come on, boys, the more you put down the more you'll pick up.
Lil Well, if 'e's runnin' this gaff, I'm 'avin' it away.

She goes for her coat

Fred Eh?
Lil (*returning*) I'm 'avin' it away, for good an' all.
Fred Yer can't do that.
Lil Oh can't I, why?
Fred 'Cause yer can't.
Lil Why.
Fred Me shirts, I mean. . . .
Lil So yer can send 'em to the laundry.
Fred Wot about when I wants a bit of . . .
Lil Yes?
Fred A bit of . . . darnin' done. Give us a kiss.
Lil Now don't be filthy.
Fred Come on, gel, give us a kiss. (*He slaps her*)
Lil If you do that again you'll 'ave to marry me.

He does it again. Rosey enters and watches

Lil Fred, will yer? Will yer, Fred? Bet yer a jacks yer wouldn't.
Fred You're on.
Rosey Oh! Lil, ain't it luvverly!
Lil (*as she goes off*) You can be my bridesmaid.
Rosey (*calling after Lil*) Lil! Is it goin' ter be a white wedding with all the trimmin's?
Lil (*returning*) Wot do yer fink? Yer 'ear that, Fred? I ain't 'avin' one of those dodgey doos down at the Town Hall.
Fred No!
Rosey Well, if Lil's gettin' married, I'm getting married. Tosher, I'm giving in my notice. Ain't it luvverly?
Tosher (*coming in*) What's lovely?
Rosey Lil and Fred. They're gettin' married.
Tosher Fred, you sure you know wot yer doin'? I mean you don't 'ave ter marry 'er. You could send 'er out to earn. I've seen worse than 'er on the bash . . . it's ridiculous.
Fred Stop rabbitin', take a tip from me. When you're on the floor, marry a whore. Get me a sky pilot.

Tosher A sky pilot? But it's legal, it's awful, it's 'orrible.
Fred Yeah, and tell 'im I want 'im right away.

Rosey starts to pack her case

Tosher (*chasing Rosey back and forth*) Wot are yer doin', Rosey?
Rosey I'm goin'. I'm goin' ter marry me boy friend. 'E gets demobbed on Thursday.
Tosher Rosey wot's the matter wiv yer?
Rosey I've 'ad enough of this sort of life, it ain't respectable and wot's more it's illegal.
Tosher Wot's illegal? Wot's the matter wiv being a brass anyway? Yer spend yer life in bed and what's more yer get paid for it.

He starts unpacking Rosey's things including false hair

Rosey I'm goin'. All I ever do is give you all the money I earn.

Tosher snatches the false hair

Eh, no, that's my false bit.
Tosher Look, I'll tell yer wot I'll do, I'll get you a nice little lumber gaff in Shepherd's Market and . . .
Rosey When?
Tosher Yeah, when. . . . Soon, and I'll getcha some new clobber and a French Maid and . . .
Rosey No, I'm definitely goin', look I've packed.
Tosher I'll sue 'im for defination of affections. . .
Rosey Well, yer can sue him for wot yer like. I'm going.
Tosher All right go.
Rosey 'Bye all, I'm stayin' for Lil's weddin' though. Ta ta, Paddy.
Tosher Don't come crawling back ter me when yer find yer've got ter do some 'ard graft out in the sticks. I just don't understand it. Ain't I always looked after 'er ever since the day she arrived on the Manor lookin' dead dodgey wiv a suitcase in 'er 'and?

Rosey crosses stage with suitcase

If it 'adn't been for me, she'd 'ave wound up posin' fer some dirty artist down in Chelsea.
Betty Do leave orf.
Tosher I don't know, I'm disgusted I am, dead disgusted.
All Oh shut up, leave off. All right, you're disgusted. . .
Tosher Fred goes straight, 'e—(*pointing at Collins*)—goes bent . . .
Collins Why don't you go down to the Oasis and observe the bird life?
Tosher Now 'e's pinchin' my lines. No matter what they say abaht that ridiculous 'at you go on wearin' it, Collins.
Collins Get out. . .

Tosher goes still muttering to himself. He gets on to the street just as a "Mystery" arrives. Betty also comes on

Tosher 'Ello, darlin'.
Mystery Hallo.
Tosher Just come up like?
Mystery Yeah, that's right.
Tosher Lookin' fer a job?
Mystery Yeah. Do you want any references?
Tosher No, but I might give yer a little audition meself.
Mystery All right.

Norman and another Ted have been watching

Norman 'Ow does 'e do it?
Tosher Well, you know the old sayin', boy, *Honi soit qui mal y ponce*, or somefing ain't it?

THE STUDENT PONCE (SONG)

Tosher

Musta' 'bin in me twenties . . .
I was a young apprentice . . .
Studied the trade . . .
Saw 'ow it paid . . .
Wanted a bit fer me
Finally found a tart who fell for me fancy style.
If I knew
Wot I *know*
I could 'ave made me pile.

Tosher, Norman, Ted

The student ponce,
Oh the student ponce
Can make a mistake
When he's not used ter countin' the take.
'E'll end up earnin' a fortune,
But only by usin' his bonce.
'E'll con if 'e don't let his girl cotton on
'E's a student ponce.

Norman and Ted

Wot if the girl yer ponce off
Suddenly finks you've gone soft . . .
Don't wanner pay . . .
'As it away . . .
Off wiv another bloke?
Wot if yer gets the needle? Wot if yer tries ter mark
The geezer,
And 'e's a
Berleedin' copper's nark?

Tosher, Norman, Ted

The student ponce,
Oh, the student ponce
Can make a mistake
When he's not used ter countin' the take.
'E'll end up earnin' a fortune,
But only by usin' his bonce.

	'E'll con if 'e don't let his girl cotton on
	'E's a student ponce.
Tosher	Hustlin' is a science . . .
	You wanner see the clients
	Comin' away . . .
	Eager ter pay . . .
	Eager ter call again.
	Amateur prostitution may be all right fer some,
	But my girls
	Are fly girls,
	And I'm so diff'rent from

Tosher, Norman,	The student ponce,
Ted	Oh, the student ponce
	Can make a mistake
	When 'e's not used ter countin' the take.
	'E'll end up earnin' a fortune,
	But only by usin' his bonce.
	'E'll con if 'e don't let his girl cotton on
	'E's a student ponce.

Tosher, Mystery, Norman and Ted go off. Enter Lil in a wedding dress, Rosey as a bridesmaid, and Redhot

Rosey A Soho weddin', isn't it romantic?
Lil What's so romantic, where's the bloody groom?

Fred enters with Paddy, sees Lil in the wedding dress and tries to run away

Collins (*coming out of the shpieler*) After him boys, bring him back. Drinks on the house. (*He toasts*) To the bride and bridegroom, may all their troubles be little ones. (*He laughs alone*)
Fred Cor where'd yer get this poison?
Collins Got it off French Herbert, we've wrapped him up as well.
Fred (*to Collins*) If I 'ad some of the gelt I've dropped you I could've a right slap up do.
Collins Trouble with you, Fred, is that you're getting mercenary in your old age.

Tosher enters followed by two Teds carrying a Priest

Lil 'Ow nice of yer to come, Farver. Wasn't it nice of 'im to come Fred?
Priest May I say, my good woman, that I have no idea what I am doing here at all. All I know is that this hooligan here came rushing into my church and dragged me out, and me in the middle of a mass for Mrs Finnegan. Who is Fred?
Fred That's me, Guv, I mean Farver.

Priest Well, what is it you want?
Fred Well, it's like this 'ere. I want ter get married like.
Priest So I can see.
Fred On the 'urry up like.
Priest You mean here, on the street?
Fred Yus.
Priest I'm afraid it's quite out of the question. If you want to get married you must come to the Church like everyone else.
Lil Oh, Farver, don't be like that, I've been tryin' ter 'ook 'im for twenty years and if I don't 'ook 'im now 'e might get away.
Priest No, I'm sorry, it's very unorthodox.
Tosher So it ain't kosher, wot's it matter?
Rosey Oh, Father, it's so nice 'ere wiv all the birds twitterin' and the patients lookin' out of the 'ospital.
Priest How long is it since you went to Confession?
Tosher Yer don't want 'er ter lose 'er 'onour now do yer?
Priest I should say it's past recovery.
Lil Wot!

The Priest starts to go but is stopped by Paddy

Paddy Here's ten pounds, Father.
Priest Oh no. . .
Paddy For the repose of the poor souls in Purgatory, Father.
Priest Oh I see. (*He pockets the money*)
Paddy And there's a bit of a hooly afterwards.
Priest This is a very solemn occasion. I think we'd better have the shortened version.
Fred Yus, make it short.
Priest Have you got any witnesses?

Fred looks around

Fred Redhot? Witness!
Redhot (*edging away*) No, I ain't never witnessed anyfink in me life and I ain't startin' now.
Fred Tosher! Witness!
Tosher Yeah, all right. (*To Priest*) But if it turns aht ter be a bent weddin' I ain't seen nuffink.
Fred Paddy. Best man.
Paddy Yes, Fred.
Lil I can't get married wivout someone ter give me away. Redhot come and give me away.
Redhot I never grassed on nobody, Lil. It's against me principles.
Lil I don't mean give me away. I mean give me 'and away.
Redhot Oh, just yer 'and like.
Lil Yes.
Redhot Oh, all right.
Priest Now, have you got a licence?
Fred No.

Priest Well, it doesn't matter.
Lil (*producing a licence*) I've got one. I've 'ad it fer ten years.
Priest Oh well, if you've got one we might as well use it.

He mumbles some of the service, then ...

Priest Do you, Frederick Cochran, take Lily Smith to be your lawful wedded wife?
Fred Yus.
Priest Do you, Lily Smith, take Frederick Cochran to be your lawful wedded husband?
Lil Yus.
Priest Have you got a ring?

Everyone looks round and Redhot brings out a trayful of rings. Fred takes one and puts it on Lil's finger

Priest I now pronounce you man and wife. Now there's the little matter of the fee.
Fred Lend us a jacks, Lil?

She gives him money and he passes it to the Priest

Priest Glory be, I'll keep the change for the christening. Is there to be any sort of celebration?
Collins Red wine for the Father.

Everyone gets a glass

P.C. enters. Collins gives him his whack

The whole cast sings

FINALE

FINGS AIN'T WOT THEY USED T'BE (REPRISE)

Here's to life within the law.
No more strife agin the law.
Fings ain't wot they used t'be.

We'll use brand new cutlery.
Oh, where can the butler be?
Fings ain't wot they used t'be.

There used to be law
Prowling around
Every place you went.
They're all on the floor—
We're underground,
How can the law stay bent?

They used to sting us—
Leave 'em well alone.
Ring us on the telephone.
Fings ain't wot they used ter—

Choose which girl yer choose ter—

Fings ain't wot they used t'be.
It used t'be fun—
Dad and ole' mum—
Paddlin' dahn Southend.
But now it ain't done.
Never mind chum,
Paris is where we spend our outings.

Monkeys flyin' rahnd the moon—
We'll be up there wiv 'em soon.
Fings ain't wot they used ter,
Did the lot we used ter,
Fings ain't wot they used t'be.

CURTAIN

PRINTED IN GREAT BRITAIN BY
THE LONGDUNN PRESS LTD., BRISTOL.